DEVELOPI
REAL WORLD
SOFTWARE

Richard Schlesinger
Kennesaw State University, Kennesaw, GA

JONES AND BARTLETT PUBLISHERS

Sudbury, Massachusetts

BOSTON   TORONTO   LONDON   SINGAPORE

World Headquarters

Jones and Bartlett Publishers
40 Tall Pine Drive
Sudbury, MA 01776
978-443-5000
info@jbpub.com
www.jbpub.com

Jones and Bartlett Publishers
Canada
6339 Ormindale Way
Mississauga, Ontario L5V 1J2
Canada

Jones and Bartlett Publishers
International
Barb House, Barb Mews
London W6 7PA
United Kingdom

Jones and Bartlett's books and products are available through most bookstores and online booksellers. To contact Jones and Bartlett Publishers directly, call 800-832-0034, fax 978-443-8000, or visit our website, www.jbpub.com.

Substantial discounts on bulk quantities of Jones and Bartlett's publications are available to corporations, professional associations, and other qualified organizations. For details and specific discount information, contact the special sales department at Jones and Bartlett via the above contact information or send an email to specialsales@jbpub.com.

Production Credits

Publisher: David Pallai
Acquisitions Editor: Timothy Anderson
Editorial Assistant: Melissa Potter
Production Director: Amy Rose
Production Assistant: Ashlee Hazeltine
Senior Marketing Manager: Andrea DeFronzo
V.P., Manufacturing and Inventory Control:
    Therese Connell

Composition: Jason Miranda / Spoke & Wheel
Art Rendering: George Nichols
Cover and Title Page Design: Kristin E. Parker
Cover and Title Page Image: © Andrea Danti/
    ShutterStock, Inc.
Printing and Binding: Malloy, Inc.
Cover Printing: Malloy, Inc.

Library of Congress Cataloging-in-Publication Data

Schlesinger, Richard, 1948-
  Developing real world software / Richard Schlesinger. – 1st ed.
      p. cm.
  Includes index.
  ISBN-13: 978-0-7637-7319-9 (pbk.)
  ISBN-10: 0-7637-7319-0 (ibid.)
  1. Computer software–Development. I. Title.
  QA76.76.D47
  005.1–dc22
                          2009021550

6048
Printed in the United States of America
13 12 11 10 09   10 9 8 7 6 5 4 3 2 1

Developing Real World Software is intended as a practical guide for developing real world software applications that are:

- *Maintainable.* Real world applications are used for many years and must be updated to fix bugs and implement new features.
- *Configurable.* Applications should be configurable to support a variety of requirements.
- *Reliable.* Real world systems should not crash or produce erroneous results. This is especially important if monetary transactions are occuring.
- *Secure.* Real world applications should be designed with the goal of preventing security attacks.

This book can serve as a useful guide for software developers who are just starting their career. It may also be used in any of the following junior- or senior-level college courses:

- Application Software Design
- Software Engineering
- Senior Project

This is not a book on the management of a software project. Many software engineering books cover that material. Similarly, many other books cover programming principles and object-oriented design. Instead, this book stresses and expands on those principles from a practical application development perspective. There is a large gap between what students typically cover in a college course and what they will see when they begin work on real applications. This book is intended to help fill that gap by tying together the various pieces of software design and programming knowledge that the reader has learned in various courses. It also covers topics such as error handling and design patterns for threads, which are often skipped in other books. While this book does not cover development frameworks such as .NET and Spring, if one understands the underlying principles found in this book it will be fairly straightforward to learn those types of systems.

The theme of proper encapsulation is carried throughout this book. While encapsulation is commonly emphasized for basic programming, this book explains how it can be used to tremendously improve the understandability and maintainability of large real world programs.

The book also shows how encapsulation applies to threads and synchronization, something that most books ignore, even though it becomes critically important in these areas.

The book uses Java and C# to illustrate the topics being discussed. However, the underlying principles can be applied to any programming language and any computer software system.

This book includes the source of a real application (client and server for a GiftCard redemption system). This system is large enough that it illustrates most of the topics covered in this book; yet, it is small enough that readers can comprehend it fairly easily. This code will be used as a case study throughout the book for examples and reader exercises.

The chapters cover the following material:

- Chapter 1 discusses project details that tend to fall in the gap between the design effort and the programming effort. This includes ensuring the application includes the tools that will enable maintainability.

- Chapter 2 covers the effects of object-oriented design on a large system. The chapter reviews some programming-style material that may have seemed interesting, but not compelling, when applied to small student programs, showing why these things are important for developing real world applications.

- Chapter 3 discusses the many aspects of making a software application configurable. This important area is typically left to on-the-job guess work. The chapter covers a number of topics including internationalization as well as how to handle requirements that change over time.

- Chapter 4 involves making sure that the system is robust and properly handles errors. This is a commonly neglected but extremely important topic, especially for any kind of transaction server.

- Chapter 5 covers material on designing for security. Readers will learn how to a Risk Analysis and then design the system to mitigate those risks. Some things that are commonly considered to be security issues are actually errors in robustness and are covered in other chapters. In early 2009, the SANS Institute (http://www.sans.org) published *The 2009 CWE/SANS 25 Most Damaging Programming Errors*. Throughout this book, recommendations are provided that concur with the SANS guidelines.

- Chapter 6 includes material on breaking a program into multiple threads. Because computers commonly have multiple processors, this is an important area for performance and responsiveness.

- Chapter 7 covers the synchronization and communication issues encountered when using multiple threads or processes. The various independent parts of an application will need to communicate with each other, and this chapter discusses how to do that correctly.

- Chapter 8 looks at how to improve the performance of an application. This is another commonly neglected but important topic. The chapter attempts to point developers in the right direction in order to obtain the best performance improvements.

- Finally, Chapter 9 covers Program Correctness and Testing. While there is much written on Software Quality Assurance testing of an entire system, there is very little on how a developer should approach analysis and testing to ensure program correctness. Thus, this chapter covers that topic, as well as overall system testing. While this chapter is last in the book, it is clearly not least important. When I teach the material in this book, I cover this chapter as soon as the students are ready to start testing their software projects.

Most of the material in this book comes from my personal experience during 30 years of managing the development of operating system components, transaction servers, communications software, and cryptographic systems. Each of the recommendations and "do not do" warnings in the book comes from seeing what worked well for me and from having to lead diagnostic teams to find and fix catastrophic problems caused when someone did not follow those warnings.

I would like to thank the Computer Science and Information Systems department at Kennesaw State University, in Kennesaw, Georgia for the support I received during the development of this book. In particular, I would like to thank my colleague Ben Setzer and the students in his Senior Project course who made important comments on an early draft of this book.

The staff at Jones and Bartlett Publishers was extremely helpful, especially Tim Anderson, Acquisitions Editor; Melissa Potter, Editorial Assistant; and Ashlee Hazeltine, Production Assistant.

Finally, I would like to thank my wife Merle and my son Ryan for their support during the development of this book.

Starting the Project

> *An application reflects the organization (and lack thereof) that created it.*

Separate people or teams of people implement real projects. Unless there is a concerted effort to provide an overall design for the application, those separately created components will not fit together well and this will be obvious to the application's users. A common example is a software system that repeatedly asks the user for his or her name and address.

Another common example of this problem is where one team develops an MS Windows version of a product while another team develops a version for Mac OS X. Often, these teams do not communicate and the result is two versions of the same product that cannot import data files from the other. This ridiculous situation can annoy customers and prevent sales.

Thus, one of the most important steps in starting a project is to create an overall design for the system(s) while ensuring good communication among the development teams.

For any significant-sized program, one should use an Object-Oriented (OO) Design methodology. This book does not cover the details of how to do Object-Oriented Design. Instead, it is assumed that an OO design has been done. However, there are many areas (such as error handling) that the design of a real-world system should include that are often neglected. These are covered in later chapters.

1.1 Plan for Maintainability

Student programs are written once and forgotten. Real-world applications are written with the intent that

1. They will be used for a long time by others.
2. Program bugs will be fixed when they are discovered.
3. Future requirement changes will be incorporated into the software.

In order for a program to be maintained (i.e., bugs fixed and new requirements incorporated) with a reasonable amount of effort, we need to plan for the *Software Development Life Cycle* (SDLC). As we proceed in implementing the development plan, we need to:

- Make sure the code is understandable when we or someone else looks at it in six months or a year. This requires using the *KISS Principle* (Keep It Simple, Stupid). While there are mathematical calculations that are extremely complex, in most cases, complicated code is an indication that the developer probably did not understand the problem well.

- Properly document the functionality of the program at all levels.

Proper object-oriented design and programming is a major step to making the code understandable. Documentation should include:

- Overall design documentation including *Unified Modeling Language* (UML) diagrams

- Detailed documentation on the program methods, their functionality, and usage

- In Java, creating Javadoc comments; using the Javadoc tool can accomplish this. In C#, you create XML comments and Visual Studio creates the documentation files.

- Comments in the code that explain the program logic and any complicated calculations

> *One of the most important features of a real-world software system are the tools you have so that when something goes wrong, you can figure out what happened.*

This is always important, but it will be critical if you do not have access to the computer that is running the software. This will be the situation in all cases except software developed solely for use within your own organization.

There are three types of tools that you should have

1. Whenever an unexplained error occurs, the software should be able to produce an *Error Report* that contains:

   a. The value of all relevant variables

   b. A *Stack Trace* that shows the sequence of method/procedure calls that caused the program to reach the point at which the error was encountered

2. The Error Report, by itself, can be used to analyze relatively simple problems. For more complicated problems, you will also need an *Event Log*. The Event Log is a file that should contain details about significant events that occurred during the execution of the program. The program should be written to record everything that happens. Ideally, the logging software

should be configurable so that you can select how much detail will actually be recorded. At a minimum, you should record every incoming and outgoing message.

3. When a serious error occurs, especially one that causes a server application to stop, it will usually be important that a notification be sent to the appropriate network operations staff. Typically, this can be done with an automated e-mail.

These tools will be valuable even during the initial development of the software. Consequently, the planning and development of these tools should be among the first things that are done in a project. Make these tools fully functional, but not overly elaborate. These tools are an example of something that adds additional upfront cost to a project, but will more than repay that cost later.

1.2 Distribution Plan

One of the topics that are often left as an afterthought is how the software will be distributed to the end-users. A plan for this should be agreed between the marketing and development teams. Questions that should be answered include:

- Will the software be provided on a CD or be downloaded from the Web (or both)?
- How will updates be provided? In today's world, it is generally expected that updates can be downloaded and installed from the Web.
- Will others be able to develop enhancements to the software? If so, you need to decide on the type of enhancements you will enable and encourage others to implement. This feature will affect the configuration options (see Section 3.4).

Regardless of how the software is distributed, you will need to provide an installation mechanism. This can be as simple as providing the software in a zip file along with instructions on how to manually perform the installation steps. However, an Installer program should be used if there are any more than a few simple installation steps.

1.3 Programming Language Selection

A very early decision in a project will be which programming language to use. Factors to consider include:

- On what type of systems will the software be installed? C# is available only for MS Windows. So, if there is the possibility that it be used on non-Microsoft systems, then another language should be chosen. Similarly, while Java is available on many systems, it is not available on all systems.

- What are the skills of the development team? Is some training required for team members?
- Are there specialized application requirements that will require using external libraries? Are these libraries available for the desired language?

1.4 Third-Party Software Selection

For every major component of the system, you will need to make a *Build vs Buy decision*. Typically, buying a software component will reduce the development time for a project. It will usually also be cheaper in the long run, but depending on the software, there may be a large upfront cost. Thus, whenever there is an available software component that meets your requirements, you should seriously consider buying it to use in a project rather than developing it yourself. The recent increased availability of open-source software means that many high-quality software components are available at minimal cost. Additionally, many companies provide a lower-end version of their commercial product at no cost. These types of products can often be a viable alternative. to an expensive purchase.

A typical large-application software system will use other software systems such as a database. The selection of these software systems will often be vital to the proper functioning of the overall system. As part of the overall system design, a number of criteria should have been developed for the overall system. These might include:

- A performance measure (such as transactions per second or response time)
- A reliability requirement for transaction integrity (see Section 4.4)

The effect of these requirements on the outside software needs to be determined and included in the selection of that software.

1.5 Tool Selection

There are a number of tools that must be selected before a project begins. A compiler and *Interactive Development Environment* (IDE) that support the desired programming language need to be selected. The development environment should fully support the language and include:

- Language-specific editing features
- If a GUI will be part of the project, there should be a good GUI layout tool
- A good interactive debugger

On a large project with many team members, it is not sufficient to just store the source code in a simple file folder. Instead, a *Source Code Management* system should be used to keep track of the various module versions created by each of the team members. Such a system allows each developer to select which version of the various modules he or she wishes to use at any moment in time. It also allows going back to a previous version if serious errors are encountered. It is highly desirable that the IDE be able to work seamlessly with the source code management system.

On a small school project, it is sufficient to interactively use the development environment to compile everything. However, on a large system, you need a Build Program that selects modules to compile based on source code changes and module dependencies. This system should be able to work with the selected source code management system. The traditional build program is called *make* and is commonly used with C++ programs. For Java development, a program called *Ant* is commonly used.

Tools for doing testing must be selected. Each different phase of testing (described in Chapter 9) will require a tool to perform the necessary exercising of the system under test.

1.6   Java and C# Features

The most common professional IDEs for Java are *Eclipse* and *NetBeans*. For C#, you will use *Microsoft Visual Studio.*

In both Java and C#, the Exception class will produce a Stack Trace when an error occurs. You will need to decide how to present the values of relevant variables. There is a Java library called *log4J* that is commonly used for creating an Event Log. A number of third-party and open-source logging tools are available for C#.

1.7   Case Study

Figure 1.1 shows the Gift Card System that we will be using as a Case Study throughout this book. In this system, there are clients located at merchants and they each connect to a server application, which in turn, is connected to a database server. The clients read a customer gift card, along with other information that the clerk enters (e.g., purchase amount) and transmits that information to the server. The server updates the card's account balance in the database. When this processing is complete, the client prints a receipt for the customer.

At first, one might think to implement the client as a simple Web applet. However, the Gift Card System was marketed to small retail stores and restaurants that typically do not have an Internet connection. Many of these stores

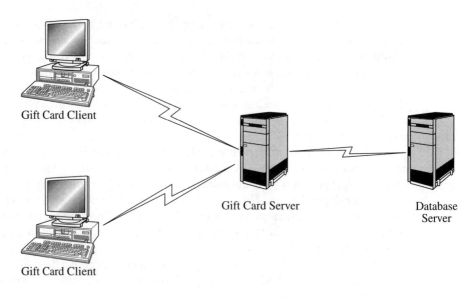

Figure 1.1   *Gift Card System*

used a hardware terminal as the client. Those stores that had a PC for their cash register used the client described here.

This Gift Card System was written in Java. Java was chosen for several reasons. The most important reason was that when the project began, it was not clear whether the server component would be running on an MS Windows computer or on a Linux computer. Using Java allowed the software to be developed and tested on Windows, and then installed on Linux when a final decision was made. In fact, the move from Windows to Linux was possible without changing any of the server code or even recompiling it.

Figure 1.2 shows the overall structure of the client. A package called GCclient contains the modules that are specific to this client application. Those modules sit on top of a communications library package. Both packages use various utility modules.

Figure 1.3 shows the overall structure of the server. A package called GCserver contains the modules that are specific to this server application. Those modules sit on top of a package that provides general support for server applications. It, in turn, sits on top of the communications library package. All of the packages use various utility modules.

The software is provided on the accompanying CD as an Eclipse Workspace that includes the source files and Javadoc files for all of these components except the Comm package. That is provided as a jar file. Installation instructions may be found in the readme file on the CD.

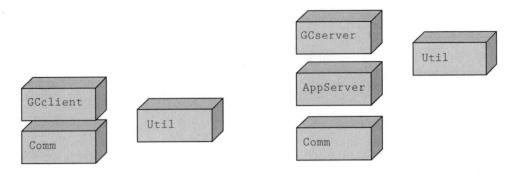

Figure 1.2   *Gift Card Client*   **Figure 1.3**   *Gift Card Server*

1.8   Exercises

1. Install the software (client, server, and database). Process some transactions using the instructions in the readme file on the CD.
2. Explore the `GCclient`, `GCserver`, and `AppServer` packages. List each module and its purpose.
3. Describe the Gift Card client's GUI.
4. Replace the logging mechanism used by the Gift Card software with calls to the log4j library.
5. Change the Gift Card server to provide a Web interface (e.g., using Tomcat and Java Server Faces [JSF]).

Object-Oriented Design and Programming

> *Confused programmers write confused programs.*

There is a relatively small amount of information that the human brain is capable of keeping track of at one time. If you go beyond that limit, you become confused (often without realizing it) and make mistakes. A real-world application will have dozens or hundreds of modules. The last thing you want to do is to search through all of the modules in a confused program to figure out what is going on. Object-Oriented Design is an attempt to minimize the confusion when developing a large program. This chapter is a review of Object-Oriented (OO) Design Principles from a perspective that is not seen in the typical OO textbook.

2.1 Abstraction and Encapsulation

The primary design concept in Object-Oriented Programming is *Abstraction*. Abstraction is the idea of hiding details when they are not needed. In particular, details of how data is maintained are hidden inside the module that contains the data. We use *Encapsulation* to implement Abstraction. Encapsulation does two things:

1. It places the code that affects data in the same module as that data.
2. It limits what other modules can do with the data.

Designing a program with proper encapsulation requires a proper *Division of Responsibility*. To do that, we need to answer the following questions:

- *Who* is responsible for maintaining each item of information? You need to decide which module will maintain each item of information.
- *What* can be done with the information? This is the set of actions (methods) that can be used on this object and provides the *Interface* for that object. If the module is a software representation of a real-world object, then the available actions should model the actions that are available in the real world.

- *When* will each of these actions be executed? In a module that represents a real-world object, this is typically determined by external events. A `BankAccount` object might have deposit and withdrawal methods that are called by a user-interface module based on user input.

- *How* will each of these methods be implemented? There can be several alternative implementations. Choosing one requires an understanding of the overall system requirements. A `BankAccount` class could store the balance simply as an instance variable in the object or it could maintain it in a database. It may even be possible that several implementations will actually be provided with one for a small system and another for a larger system. Which one is actually used would be a configuration option (see Chapter 3, Configurable Applications).

So, why is proper encapsulation so important? Two things happen when we do proper encapsulation.

1. We are better able to infer *Program Correctness* (see Chapter 9).

2. We tend to isolate problems to a single module rather than having them propagated throughout the program.

When we do a Division of Responsibility, we need to keep the KISS Principle in mind. Let's take a look at the code in Example 2.1. In this example, the main method (`insertTransaction`) creates a `GiftCard` object and passes in a parameter indicating whether the card account must already exist. `GiftCard` determines whether the card already exists and retains state information (`existingCard`) that is used later when its update method is called.

Now, compare that code with the code in Example 2.2 in which the responsibilities have been divided between the two modules in a much simpler fashion. In this example, the `GiftCard` class does not care whether the card previously existed. All of the logic related to that is retained in the `insertTransaction` method. While this makes `insertTransaction` somewhat more complicated, the overall effect is simpler because you do not have to constantly look back and forth at the two modules to understand what is happening.

By following these guidelines, a properly encapsulated program will tend to isolate each problem to a single module. Otherwise, errors will tend to be propagated throughout a large system. In fact, we can measure this.

2.2 Reference Complexity

The *data reference complexity* of a primitive variable (e.g., number, boolean, character) is the number of modules that access or change that variable. In a properly encapsulated module, the data reference complexity of each variable is one (i.e., the module that contains the data item). Thus, you only need to look at that single module to see what changes can possibly be made to the data of that module. In a poorly encapsulated program, you have to closely examine

```
public double redeem(Transaction t)
     throws InvalidAccountException, {

     double balance = 0.0;
     // Get Gift Card (must already exist)

     GiftCard gc = new GiftCard(cardNumber, true);
     balance = gc.redeem(amount);

     gc.update();
     return balance;
}


public class GiftCard extends SQLDB {
     private static enum FIELDS {CardNumber, Balance};
     private boolean existingCard;
     public GiftCard(String cardNumber, boolean cardMustExist)
             throws InvalidAccountException {

         super(FIELDS.class);

         String query1 = "SELECT * FROM GiftCards WHERE
                 CardNumber='" + cardNumber + "'";
         // Find the card (if it exists)
         executeQuery(query1);
         if (isEmpty()) {
             if (cardMustExist)
                 throw new InvalidAccountException();
             existingCard = false;
         }
         else {
             existingCard = true;
         }
     }
     //////////////////////////////////////////////////////////////////
     public void update() {
         if (existingCard)
             super.update();
         else
             super.insert();
```

Example 2.1   *Complicated Division of Responsibility*

```
private double redeem(Transaction t)
        throws InvalidAccountException {
    double balance = 0.0;

    // Find record for this card
    GiftCard gc = new GiftCard(cardNumber);
    // Using the card; it must already exist
    if (gc.isEmpty()) {
        throw new InvalidAccountException();
    }
    // Decrement balance on card and update its record
    balance = gc.redeem(amount);
    gc.update();
}


public class GiftCard extends SQLDB {
    private static enum FIELDS {CardNumber, Balance};

    public GiftCard(String cardNumber) {
        super(FIELDS.class);
        String query1 = "SELECT * FROM GiftCards WHERE
                CardNumber='" + cardNumber + "'";
        executeQuery(query1);
    }
}
```

Example 2.2 *Simpler Division of Responsibility*

all of the modules that reference this module's data to see what changes they are making to the data.

It is important to understand that it is not enough to simply declare instance variables to be private and then define *getter* and *setter* methods for those variables. To be properly encapsulated, the calculations that compute new values for instance variables should be in the module with the data. Otherwise, you still need to examine all of the referencing modules to determine the possible changes to a variable. Additionally, one should have a setter method for a variable only if it is truly necessary to set arbitrary values for that variable at arbitrary times during the program execution. In Example 2.3, the Circle class is poorly encapsulated. One has to look at the modules that use Circle to determine that the calculations for area and circumference are being done incorrectly.

```
public class Main {
    double radius;

    Circle c = new Circle();
    c.setArea(2 * Math.PI * radius);
    c.setCircumference(Math.PI * radius * radius);


}

public class Circle {
    private double radius;
    private double area;
    private double circumference;

    public void setArea(double value) {
        area = value;
    }

    public void setCircumference(double value) {
        circumference = value;
    }
}
```

Example 2.3   *Poor Encapsulation*

In Example 2.4, one only needs to look inside the `Circle` class to determine the incorrect calculations.

It is actually not necessary for the `Circle` class to maintain variables for area and circumference because those values can be easily calculated from the radius. Example 2.5 shows the improved version of the `Circle` class.

When one starts dealing with *reference variables* (i.e., variables that reference other objects), the situation gets exponentially more complex. The *static reference complexity* of a module is equal to the number of other modules that reference this module times the number of other modules this module references. In Figure 2.1, module abc references three modules and four modules reference it. Its reference complexity is 12.

In a program without proper encapsulation, each module will have a very high reference complexity. Why is this important? For all but the most trivial of errors, finding an error in a poorly encapsulated program will require looking

Encapsulation is the Object-Oriented Programming feature that makes large programs manageable.

```
public class Main {
    double radius;

    Circle c = new Circle();
    c.setArea(radius);
    c.setCircumference(radius);
}

public class Circle {
    private double radius;
    private double area;
    private double circumference;

    public void setArea(double radius) {
        area = 2 * Math.PI * radius;
    }

    public void setCircumference(double radius) {
        circumference = Math.PI * radius * radius;
    }
}
```

Example 2.4   *Better Encapsulation*

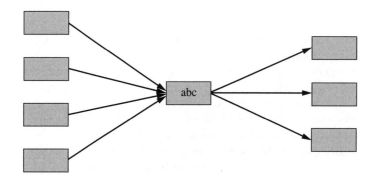

Figure 2.1   *Static Reference Complexity*

at all combinations of usage of the module or modules one is concerned about. In other words, the larger the reference complexity, the more time and effort will be expended to figure out and fix the problem. Furthermore, an extremely large reference complexity can actually tax the ability of the human mind to comprehend what is happening. This, in turn, means a less robust program.

```
public class Main {
    double theRadius;

    Circle c = new Circle(theRadius);
}

public class Circle {
    private double radius;

    public circle(double radius) {
        this.radius = radius;
    }

    public void getArea() {
        return Math.PI * radius * radius;
    }

    public void getCircumference() {
        return 2 * Math.PI * radius;
    }
}
```

Example 2.5 *Best Encapsulation*

On the other hand, in a properly encapsulated program, you can take advantage of each module's inferred correctness to limit how much of the program you need to examine to find a problem.

2.3 Inheritance and Interfaces

Inheritance and Interfaces provide similar functionality. So how do you decide which one to use? There is a natural temptation to use Inheritance as it allows one to construct rather complex class structures. Interfaces give you only a flat structure. However, most programming languages have a restriction that a class can inherit from only one other class (but one class can implement multiple Interfaces). Thus, it can easily be the case that you start constructing several complex Inheritance structures and then find that you need to create a class that Inherits from multiple other classes. At that point, you find yourself tearing down everything you created to restructure it in the form of Interfaces. Consequently, it is prudent to carefully design these structures so that they are generally useful.

A general rule to follow is that it is OK to use Inheritance if the base class provides significant functionality that will be used by the subclasses. Otherwise, an Interface is a better approach.

Encapsulation with Inheritance is problematic. This is because encapsulation says to enclose things into one module, but Inheritance says that subclasses can affect the underlying base class. So, we are back to looking at more than one module to understand what is happening. At least, the additional affected modules are limited to the subclasses of the base class. Let's examine two different cases.

If all of the instance variables in the base class are *private*, then the subclasses can only add functionality without affecting the underlying features of the base class. Notice that even if a subclass overrides a method from the base class, it cannot directly affect the underlying functionality because it has no access to the base class's instance variables. In this case, everything we have discussed about encapsulation still applies.

A common approach to implementing a class hierarchy is to simply declare all of the base class's instance variables to be *protected* (i.e., subclasses can directly change those variables). This allows the subclasses to affect the base class's underlying functionality. It is this case that requires understanding all of the subclasses to understand what is happening. Since the subclass hierarchy tree (Figure 2.2) can be quite large, this situation can become unwieldy very quickly. Thus, the use of protected instance variables should be avoided if at all possible.

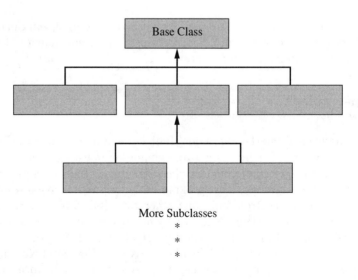

More Subclasses

*

*

*

Figure 2.2   *Class Hierarchy*

2.4 Database Access

SQL is a straight-line procedural language. Consequently, there is a tendency to implement the database accesses from a program in a strictly procedural manner. Unfortunately, this often leads to very convoluted code. A better approach is to represent each database table as a class in the program. More particularly, each object will represent one or more records from that table.

In this approach, each class will have:

- Constructors
  - A constructor for creating a record that will be inserted into the table after its fields have been properly filled in.
  - One or more constructors that have search criteria as parameters will create an object that represents the results of the associated query.
- Getters and Setters
  - One might be tempted to have the getters and setters directly access the fields in the data record rather than have separate instance variables. That is OK except that some databases do not like one to retrieve a value from a record that has not yet been inserted into the database. Another approach is to maintain a write-through cache of the field values (see Section 8.4).
  - Note that this is an excellent example of using the getters and setters to hide how the data is actually being stored.
- Other Methods
  - Insert to insert a new record.
  - Update to write out changed values for a record.
  - Navigation methods (e.g., next) to move among the records that have satisfied the search criteria.

Figure 2.3 illustrates this idea.

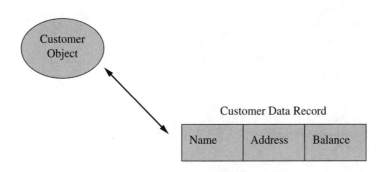

Figure 2.3   *Database Object*

2.5 Using UML

So far in this chapter, we have considered the static analysis that one sees in a *UML Class Diagram*. However, to do a complete design analysis, one also needs to look at the dynamic aspects of the system. The *UML State Change Diagram* and *UML Sequence Diagram* are useful in understanding the internal structure and activity of the various classes. We shall use the *UML Collaboration Diagram* for Error Analysis (Chapter 4), Parallel Processing Analysis (Chapter 6), and Synchronization Analysis (Chapter 7).

2.6 Some Guidelines

When writing a properly encapsulated program, one should do the following:

1. In student assignments, you probably used type double (or float) to represent money. Unfortunately, these types can have rounding errors that can create inexact results. Therefore, in real applications, you should use a type that always produces exact answers (such as a decimal-based type).

2. Whenever possible, use named constants or enumeration sets. These will have a number of effects:

   a. It will convert simple typing mistakes from hard-to-find runtime errors into easy to fix compile-time errors.

   b. Six months or a year later, when you or someone else is looking at the code, you won't have to scratch your head as to why some literal constant was used at this spot. The meaning of the named constant will be self-explanatory. Compare Examples 2.6 and 2.7. Which is easier to understand what is happening?

```
if (transactionType==5) {
    // Misc code
}
```

Example 2.6   *Named Constant Not Used*

```
if (transactionType==NEW_INVESTMENT) {
    // Misc code
}
```

Example 2.7   *Named Constant Used*

c. If the value of a named constant needs to change, you won't have to search through the entire program finding all the places that value is used and each time wondering whether that value refers to this particular usage. You will only need to change the value in one place.

Not only should you use named constants and enumerations in a single program, this is an especially valuable thing to do for values that will be used in messages between separate processes. Establish a library directory of these constants that can be used by all components. However, be careful of the issues discussed in Section 3.3.

3. Never use *public* instance variables. These violate encapsulation and are an invitation to make a mess of your program.

4. Any outside objects that are needed by an object should be created by that object or passed to it (typically in the constructor).

5. While it is common to use *public static final* to define constants, you should never use *public static variables*. Not only will they make a mess of your program, but in a multi-threaded application, their use can also create *race conditions*. (See Chapter 7).

6. It might seem sexy to have your problem dynamically create its own code on the fly. Unfortunately this is extremely error-prone and can easily lead to security problems because it allows an attacker to completely control your program.

Both Java and C# allow the developer to do proper encapsulation, but it is not required. Many developers do not do proper encapsulation because at first glance, it appears to take more effort. Certainly, it does take more effort in the design and coding. However, that up-front effort is more than repaid in reducing the effort to discover and fix problems later.

2.7 Java and C# Features

Java and C# include the standard Object-Oriented Programming features:

- Classes
- Inheritance, Interfaces, and Polymorphism
- Scope Modifiers (public, private, protected)

In Section 2.3, Inheritance, it was noted that the use of the *protected* visibility modifier made it more difficult to understand the overall operation of the classes, but one needed only to examine the subclasses of a class to understand the effects. In Java (but not C#), the protected modifier makes a variable visible to all of the classes in a package, thus potentially greatly increasing the number of modules that must be examined and understood.

Java has a library class, *BigDecimal*, which can be used to represent monetary values. Similarly, C# has a *decimal* type that can be used for these types of values.

Java supports a feature known as *JDBC* (Java Database Connectivity). There is a JDBC driver for every database engine (e.g., Oracle, SQL Server, MYSQL). With a JDBC driver for the particular database engine you are using, you can then access the database using SQL statements.

JDBC works with the object structure shown in Figure 2.4. The Database Driver provides one or more Connection objects, representing the connection to the database (which might be on another machine across the Internet). Each of the Connection objects can have one or more Statement objects, which represent SQL statements. Each Statement object will have one Result Set, representing the data rows (records) provided by the SQL statement. One can then access the record fields from the Result Set. It is also possible to update fields in the Result Set and have the updated record written to the database.

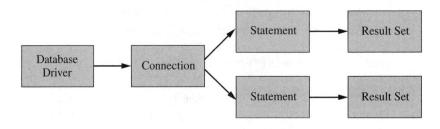

Figure 2.4   *Java JDBC Structures*

Example 2.8 shows a simple example of using the JDBC interface to access a database.

```
// Locate the database driver for this particular JDBC interface
Class.forName(JdbcDriver);

// Get a Connection object from the database driver
Connection conn = DriverManager.getConnection(jdbcUrl, userId,
    password);

// Create Statement object that allows scrolling thru results
//and also allows the database to be updated
Statement dbStatement =
    conn.createStatement(ResultSet.TYPE_SCROLL_SENSITIVE,
    ResultSet.CONCUR_UPDATABLE);

// Perform the query and return the results
ResultSet rs = dbStatement.executeQuery(sql);
```

Example 2.8   *Sample JDBC Usage*

C# provides support for *ADO.NET*, which provides a similar level of functionality to JDBC. It includes classes that provide more efficient access to SQL Server and Oracle databases. Additionally, the .NET Language Integrated Query Framework (*LINQ*) provides classes that perform the Object to SQL table mapping that was recommended in this section. Visual Studio includes a tool that simplifies creating this mapping.

2.8   Case Study

The Application Server (AppServer) contains three classes that serve as a foundation for database access:

- SQLDB manages `Connection` objects and performs SQL queries. Since the Application Server can run multiple simultaneous transactions, each with a separate thread, SQLDB is written so that there will be a separate `Connection` object for each thread.

- `DataRecord` is a base class for objects that will represent a record in a database table. It includes a write-through cache for the fields in the record. It also includes Insert and Update functionality.

- `DataRecordGroup` is a base class that will represent a group of records (selected by a query). It includes the ability to navigate through the group, with each movement returning a `DataRecord`.

The Gift Card server has a database with three tables (`Merchants`, `GiftCards`, and `Transactions`). The Java code has corresponding classes (`Merchant`, `GiftCard`, and `Transaction`). Each of those classes extends the `DataRecord` class. There is also a class called `TransactionGroup` that represents a set of records from the `Transactions` table. It extends the `DataRecordGroup`.

The Gift Card software uses its own library class, `Money`, which is a wrapper around BigDecimal that also provides various formatting methods.

Figure 2.5 shows the classes in the GiftCard Client.

- The GUI class is the main user interface to the program. It calls upon `ConfigurationGUI` if a configuration change is desired. It will use the `GiftCard` and `NumericKeyPad` classes to build the frame that is displayed for the user.

- `MSRField` is a class that will parse the data that is read from the magnetic stripe of a card or typed by the clerk. `PrivateCard` is a subclass that understands the particular format of the data on a Private Label Card such as this Gift Card.

- `NumericKeyPad` presents a numeric keypad on the screen. This is necessary to support systems that have touch screen monitors and no keyboard or mouse.

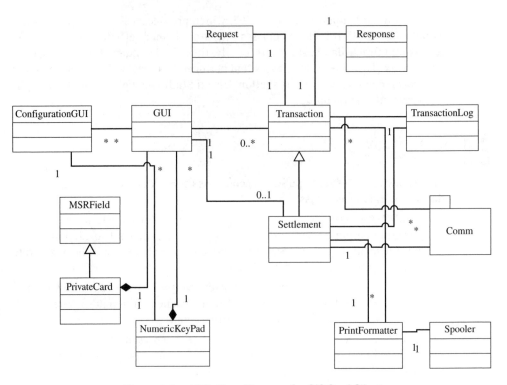

Figure 2.5 *UML Class Diagram for GiftCard Client*

- If the clerk requests that a transaction be processed, the `Transaction` class is instantiated to handle the request. It will use the `PrintFormatter` to create a receipt for the customer. Finally, it will record itself in the `TransactionLog`.

- If the clerk wishes to settle the day's transactions, the GUI will instantiate the `Settlement` class. It will read the day's transactions from the `TransactionLog` and use the `PrintFormatter` to produce a Settlement Report.

- Both the `Transaction` and `Settlement` classes use the `Comm` package to communicate with the GiftCard Server.

Figure 2.6 shows the classes in the Application Server.

- `TransactionServer` does some basic initialization and then starts the `ApplicationLayerFactory`.

- The `ApplicationLayerFactory` will start one or more instances of the `ApplicationLayer`, each of which is a separate thread. These threads will handle the processing of requests coming into the server.

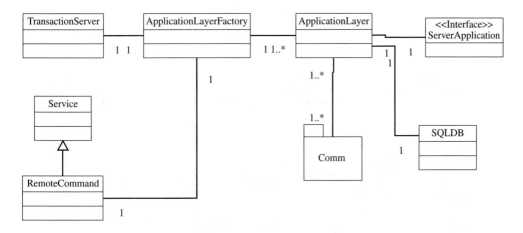

Figure 2.6 *UML Class Diagram for Application Server*

- The `ApplicationLayer` uses the `Comm` package to receive transaction requests and send responses. Whenever a request arrives, it calls a `ServerApplication`.
- Potential applications must conform to the `ServerApplication` interface. The actual class to be instantiated is specified as a configuration parameter.

Figure 2.7 shows the classes for the GiftCard Server application

- TerminalTransaction implements the `ServerApplication` interface defined by the Application Server. It is the main transaction processing class for this server.
- The `Request` class represents a request message from a client to the server. It includes an Enumeration for the types of requests. The `Response` class represents a response message from the server back to the client. It includes an enumeration for the response codes.
- `TerminalTransaction` instantiates objects to represent records in the database.
    - `Merchant` represents a record in the Merchants table.
    - `GiftCard` represents a record in the GiftCard table.
    - `Transaction` represents a record from the Transactions table.
    - `TransactionGroup` represents a set of transaction records.
    - If the transaction is to initialize a client, then `TerminalTransaction` instantiates `TerminalInitializer`, which in turn, uses `PCInitializer` to send data to the client PC.

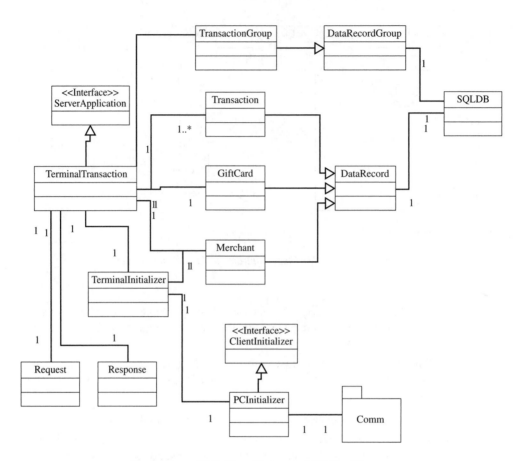

Figure 2.7 *UML Class Diagram of GiftCard Server*

2.9 Exercises

1. Explain in detail the functionality provided by each of the database interface modules `SQLDB`, `DataRecord`, and `DataRecordGroup`. These modules are in the GiftCard software's `AppServer` package.

2. In the Gift Card client, the `Transaction` module has a number of instance variables that are declared as protected. Explain how this affects understanding what goes on in this module and its subclass `Settlement`.

3. In the `AppServer` package, the `DataRecord` and `DataRecordGroup` classes have no protected fields. How does this impact their subclasses? Contrast this with the Transaction module in the Gift Card client.

Configurable Applications

> *The only constant is change.*

Most applications should have configuration options. These allow one application to serve many similar but slightly different marketing and/or user requirements. Examples of configuration options include:

- The name of the business that is using the software
- The hostname of a server to be used
- How many simultaneous requests to support
- What language to use for messages

At design time, one needs to decide on the configuration options. Then, one should decide which configuration options the end-user can select and which options a system administrator should select. A GUI should be provided for all configuration options that are user selectable. For configuration options that a system administrator selects, it is a marketing decision as to whether a GUI is necessary. Configuration parameters can also be downloaded from another system or negotiated with another system.

There are two common approaches to storing configuration parameters:

1. Parameters are stored in a "properties" file. Each parameter is typically recorded in the file in a format such as:

    <Parameter Name> = <Value>

2. MS Windows has a *Registry* for storing configuration options. Figure 3.1 shows a portion of a registry. The Registry is a multi-rooted tree structure with sub-keys and values at each level of the tree. Most of it is used by the Windows operating system for its own configuration parameters. However, there is a section shown in the figure where applications can store their own configuration parameters. An application can place its own configuration parameters at

    HKEY_LOCAL_MACHINE\Software\<Vendor Name>\<Application Name>

Where <Vendor Name> is the name of the company that created the software, and <Application Name> is the name of the particular application.

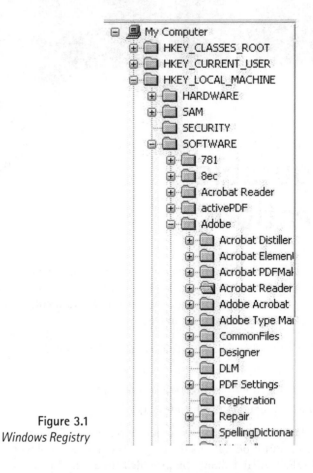

Figure 3.1
Windows Registry

The Windows Registry is OS-specific. Consequently, any application that is intended to run on more than one operating system (OS) should use the Windows Registry only for things that are required by the Windows operating system.

Beware that a poor decision about where to store configuration information can inadvertently cause a security vulnerability. See Section 5.3 for details. It is critical that you ensure that all system parameters have been properly set up in the initialization of the program. Be sure to do data validity testing (Section 4.2) on all configuration parameters.

3.1   Factory Classes

For many configuration options, it is simply a matter of storing and using the user-specified number or string. However, there are other configuration options that require a decision about which one of several polymorphic classes to instantiate. That is the job of a *factory class*.

A factory class will use parameters (either passed to it or that it finds in a configuration file) to decide which one of several classes to instantiate. Each of the possible candidate classes provides the same programmatic interface, but implements that interface differently. Thus, they are polymorphic. Either they all are subclasses of the same base class or they all implement the same Interface. An example might be a set of communication classes. Each one implements a different communication protocol (e.g., TCP/IP, X.25, dialup), but each can be used in the same manner to communicate with another system.

There are two approaches to implementing a factory class:

- In the first approach, one simply has a sequence of if statements to determine which class to instantiate. This is simple, but it requires that all of the potential classes that could be instantiated be compiled with the factory. Example 3.1 shows such a factory. The method `getReport` receives a string parameter that indicates which class is to be instantiated. All of the classes that can be instantiated either are subclasses of a class called `Report`, or they all implement an interface called `Report`.

- In the second approach, one uses the programming language's *reflection* features to find and instantiate a class that need not be compiled with the factory. The reflection features in Java and C# allow a program to examine and use the internal structures in an object module. This approach is more general and allows the development of classes to be done separately from the development of the main program. See Example 3.2.

```
public class ReportFactory
{
    public static Report getReport(String reportType)
    {
        if (reportType.equals("Monthly")
        {

            return new MonthlyReport();
        }
        else if
        {
            return new AnnualReport();
        }
    }
}
```

Example 3.1 *Simple Factory Class*

```
public class ReportFactory
{
    public static Report getReport(String reportType)
    {
        // Get Class for this report
        Class c0 = Class.forName(reportType);

        // Instantiate the class
        return c0.newInstance();
    }
}
```

Example 3.2 *More General Factory Class*

3.2 Internationalization

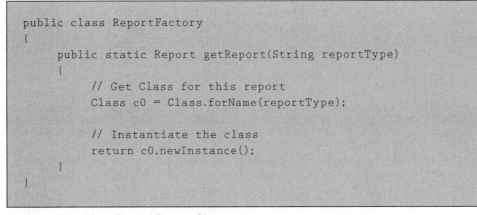

In the 21st century, being successful means being international.

In today's world, many applications must meet international requirements.

- The software may be sold in several countries
- The software may be used by a multinational company with offices in multiple countries.
- The software may need to work with files created using another language.
- The software may need to support multiple languages in a single country.

Thus, there may be a varying set of requirements that include:

- Support for different time zones and time-of-day and date formats. Some countries use a 24-hour time-of-day format. There are various different date formats in different countries. The U.S. format is typically Month–Day–Year. In many countries, it is Day–Month–Year.
- Support for different currency formats. Countries have different currencies. There are different currency symbols and different ways to represent the currency amounts.
- Support for files in non-English languages.
- Provide a user interface in a non-English language.

The standard PC character set supports the western European languages. To support other languages, you should use the Unicode character set. Java and C# natively use Unicode. If you are programming in C++, you will need to use wide characters for Unicode.

There are two basic concepts that are used to support internationalization. The first is the concept of *Locale*. A locale is the combination of a country and a language. For example, both English and French are used in Canada. Thus, there are two locales:

- Canada, English
- Canada, French

While there are typically predefined locales, you can also create your own as needed. For example, we commonly think of the United States English as a locale. However, a specialized application might create a locale with the United States and another language.

Each locale has a defined format for time-of-day, dates, and currency.

The second concept for Internationalization is that all information that is Locale-specific is placed into a separate *Resource File*. This will include the text of messages, possibly icons, and so on.

Thus, Internationalization consists of

- Using Locale-dependent formatters for time-of-day, date, and currency
- Defining the information to be in a Resource File and accessing that information from the Resource File, rather than as literal strings in the program

Localization consists of creating a Resource File for a specific locale. This can be done as a process completely separate from the development of the program code. This separation of Internationalization from Localization also models the skills of the people doing the work. Typically, a software developer will not be fluent in all of the desired languages. Thus, professional language translators will usually create the resource files for additional locales.

It will be a management decision as to whether to build multiple software packages, each with support for a separate locale or one package that can select the locale to be used during installation or at runtime. If the package includes support for more than one locale, then the typical software will default to use the locale defined for the operating system on which the software is installed.

Both Java and C# have built-in features to support these requirements.

3.3 Message Protocols

Any software system that has components distributed across multiple computers will need a facility to have those components communicate with each other. That means that application message formats and protocols need to be designed. Just as the software components will evolve over time, the message formats (and possibly the protocol) will also evolve. Examples include:

- A new value will be defined for a field.
- A new field will be defined.

This type of change means that every message should include a *version-identifier* field, indicating which message format is being used.

As the new message formats and protocols evolve, new versions of the message-handling classes also need to be developed. Do *not* completely replace an old message-handling class with a new one. That will have the effect of requiring that all computers be simultaneously updated with the new software. This is a logistical nightmare that cannot work on anything other than the smallest networks.

Instead, the software will need to support multiple message formats (and protocols) and have a factory class instantiate the appropriate one based on what is actually needed. Notice that this requirement to support older message protocols also means that when a system is communicating with another that uses an older protocol, the functionality provided by the newer protocol will not be available. The overall system must be designed to comprehend this situation.

To determine which format/protocol is needed, a negotiation protocol should be used. There are two common ones:

- The first is really an operational procedure rather than a software protocol. Install the upgraded software on all of the receivers before it is installed on any of the senders. That way, senders can always use the latest protocol that they know about. This can work on small networks or on systems with a single server. However, if a system is sometimes a sender and sometimes a receiver, this procedure will not work.

- The better procedure is a software negotiation protocol. The sender first sends a message listing all of the formats/protocols that it supports. The receiver matches those against what it supports and sends back a message saying which format/protocol to use. See Figure 3.2.

The best way to implement the handling of a changing message protocol is to encapsulate the code for the message handling for both the sender and the receiver in a single class. This is illustrated in Example 3.3.

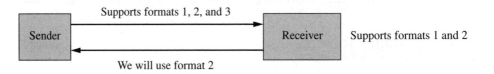

Figure 3.2   *Message Format Negotiation*

```
Constructor used by sender. It takes various parameter values
and stores them into instance variables
  .

  .
toString method. Used by sender to format string for
transmission to receiver.
  .

  .
Constructor used by receiver. It parses the received string and
places values into instance variables
  .

  .
Getters. Used by the receiver to obtain the individual
parameter values.
```

Example 3.3   *Encapsulation of a Message*

3.4 External Enhancements

Depending on the type of software and the marketing plan, a highly desirable feature will be the ability of others outside the original development team to develop enhancements (also known as add-ins) to the software. Common examples of this are

- Others will develop the Resource File to support an additional language.
- Another company might create a module that produces a new type of report.
- Someone will create a module for saving the program's data in a different format.

   If this type of feature is to be supported, then you must:

- Provide "hooks" in the software to enable external enhancements to interface with the main application.
- Provide sufficient documentation to enable others to develop the enhanced features.
- Provide a mechanism to determine what (if any) enhancements are installed. This could either be parameters in a configuration file or an automatic search for modules installed in a specified location. Note that the search path should be carefully controlled as it can be used by an attacker to corrupt your program.
- To actually use independently developed modules, you will need factory classes to instantiate those modules.

If you are developing an application that will be used in a large enterprise, then you probably should implement the modules that produce the Event Log and send mail in case of a significant error as external enhancements. You should provide default modules for this functionality but allow the enterprise IT staff the ability to create customized modules that will integrate into their network management systems.

3.5 Licensing Restrictions

If this software is being sold, one of the marketing requirements may be to include licensing restrictions. Licensing restrictions will restrict who can install the software and/or what functionality is provided by the installed software. Common examples include:

- Anti-piracy provisions such as requiring that a key be entered when the software is installed
- Limiting the number of simultaneous users (based on how much the customer has paid)
- Limiting how long certain functionality will work. This typically requires the customer to buy a subscription to continue the working functionality. An example is anti-virus programs, which require a subscription to continue receiving updates.

If there are licensing restrictions, there will typically be a requirement to implement them so that they cannot be easily bypassed. Customers are very clever and most homegrown licensing restrictions eventually are bypassed. One should give serious consideration to the Build vs Buy decision on this type of requirement.

3.6 Help Files

A modern application will include most of its end-user documentation as online help files. This can be done either as files included with the software package or as a link to files on a Web server. In either case, search functionality should be included. Since this is end-user documentation, it should adapt to the Locale that is being used by the end-user.

Typically, a technical writer creates the Help files. There are a number of Help file creation tools available. These tools will format the files and include a search mechanism for the end-user. The software development team needs to

- Explain the system and its usage to the technical writer
- Include the mechanism for the user to invoke the help component

3.7   Installing Updates

The process of installing updates is a form of reconfiguration of the application. How this can be done will depend on

- The operating system
- The type of application. Updating a constantly running program (such as a Web server) is different from updating an end-user (client) program
- The language the program is written in

3.8   Java and C# Features

Java has a *Properties class* that can be used to handle configuration parameters. A Properties object will have an associated file from which configuration parameters can be read and written. Configuration parameters in the file will be of the form:

```
⟨name⟩ = ⟨value⟩
```

The Properties File can also be in XML format. If you are using the Windows Registry, there is a third-party library available to allow access from Java.

C# applications can store configuration parameters in a .config file, whose values can be set on the end-user system with a .NET tool that works within the Administrative Tools application. A C# program can use the *Registry* and *RegistryKey* classes to access the Windows Registry.

Java has a *DateFormat* class that will handle the formatting of dates and time of day according to a specified (or default) Locale. Similarly, the *NumberFormat* class has a getCurrencyInstance method that will return a formatter object for the currency in the specified (or default) Locale.

C# uses a *NumberFormatInfo* structure to describe how numbers should be formatted for a particular Locale (aka Culture). The *ToString* method optionally accepts a Culture parameter to define how formatting should be performed.

The Java *ResourceBundle* class provides the mechanism for handling a Resource File. In C#, the *ResourceManager* class provides similar functionality.

Both Java and C# have reflection features that can be used to enable most external enhancements.

Java has a facility that allows you to write an object to a file and later instantiate it from the data in the file. Do not attempt to use this feature as a mechanism to communicate data between systems. Doing this requires that *all* systems be simultaneously updated to the same software level; thus, creating major logistical problems.

3.9 Case Study

The Util package has a Profile class that was created before the Java Properties class existed. Profile includes support for integer and Boolean parameters. A profile object also has a prefix string that automatically preceeds any name provided to the Profile object. This provides a simple mechanism to have a group of related properties (e.g., Net.port and Net.hostname).

The GiftCard client includes a GUI for setting configuration parameters. There is also a feature for having some configuration parameters downloaded to the client from the server. The GiftCard client supports receipt printers that are directly connected to the PC running the client. It also supports a DebugPrinter class that displays the receipt in a window on the screen. The software on the CD is configured to use the DebugPrinter. Most small retail stores and restaurants do not have Internet access. Consequently, the client supports using a dialup connection to the GiftCard server as well as using an Internet connection. The dialup feature is disabled in the software on the CD.

A Java ResourceBundle object will throw an Exception if an attempt is made to access a resource that is not in that particular Resource File. The GiftCard client has its own Resource class that catches that exception and uses the English language resource file in that situation. The application was deployed only in the United States; so it does not take advantage of any internationalization features for data and currency formats.

The client and server encapsulate the Request and Response messages in separate classes. This isolates the message formats and facilitates the formats changing over time. The message formats used in this application include a version identifier. Since there was only a single server and the rest of the system consists of simple clients, the procedural approach was used for negotiating message format and protocol.

The client will display a simple text file to provide help for a clerk who is not familiar with the application.

3.10 Exercises

1. Describe the Configuration GUI in the GiftCard client.

2. Describe the configuration profile mechanism used by both the GiftCard client and server.

3. Document in detail how Java or C# Resource Files are formatted, named, and selected for use.

4. The Gift Card software includes a resource for French language (The actual file contains English text preceded by the letter *f*.) Change the configuration for the client to specify French language. Confirm that this change functions correctly.

5. Consider an enhancement to the messaging protocol between the GiftCard client and server so that it uses the negotiation protocol described in Section 3.3. Write pseudo code (or another description) of how this would work.

6. Replace the configuration files used by the GiftCard system with an XML structure.

7. Change the message format between the GiftCard client and server to use XML.

Error Handling and Robustness

> *In the real world, the abnormal will be normal.*

Robustness is an attribute of a program that indicates how well it handles abnormal situations. Unfortunately, many developers do one of the following:

- Ignore the abnormal situations completely
- Consider them only as an afterthought
- Only consider a small subset of the abnormal situations

There is a variant of "Murphy's Law" that says that whatever abnormal situations you ignored during the design of a program will actually occur during production usage of the application. Consequently, a thorough understanding of the abnormal situations must be considered as part of the main design and development effort.

Errors fall into several classes:

- *Data Validity Errors*, in which data received from the outside world does not follow the expected syntax. This is discussed in detail in Section 4.2.
- *Semantic Errors*, in which the external request function cannot or should not be performed (e.g., user asks to withdraw more money than is in the account).
- *Configuration Errors*, in which the software is not prepared for a request. Examples include things such as a client not having a server system specified. These types of errors typically result in "See System Administrator" messages.
- *Programming Errors*, in which an error in the programming causes completely unexpected results.
- *System Failures*, in which the computing system is not functioning properly.

4.1 Error Handling

What do you do when an error occurs? The answer to this question can get rather complicated because of where knowledge is available in the program. At the point where the error is actually detected, you have very detailed information about the error itself, but often very little information about the context in which the error occurred (e.g., What was the user doing?). On the other hand, at the point where you have the contextual information, you tend to not know much about the specifics of the error.

The result of this is that we often see two kinds of error messages:

- SQL Driver Error 59834
- Unable to process user request

The first type of error message provides all of the specific error information, but no context. Consequently, it will be indecipherable for the typical user. The second type of message provides the context, but no information about what the error actually was. Neither of these types of error messages is really useful. To properly handle this situation, you need to

1. Propagate the error upwards in the call stack (back to whoever called this routine).

2. At each level of the call stack, transform the error information into something that is relevant to that context.

Let's look at the example in Figure 4.1:

1. The user enters his or her name to log on to the system.

2. The system passes the request down several levels of method calls to the point that it accesses a database.

3. The database returns the specific error "Query Failed." Is that an appropriate message to report to the user? It is better to pass that error up the call stack until we reach the point that we understand what was being queried. At that point, we can report the error "Name not found."

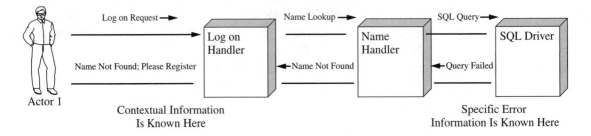

Figure 4.1 *Error Understanding*

4. However, while we now understand that it was the name that was not found, at this level we may not know why the name was being queried. So, we need to pass the error up the call stack again until we understand that the user was attempting to log on to his or her account. Now, we can report "Name not found. Please register" (or whatever might be appropriate for the situation).

This example illustrates that at the top of the method call stack, one has great contextual knowledge (what the user is doing), but little knowledge about the specifics of an error that will be detected many layers deep in the call tree. At the bottom of the call stack, the error is detected and you have great knowledge about its specifics, but you have lost the contextual knowledge. Thus, we have the requirement to pass the error up the call stack and change it at each level to match the contextual knowledge at that level.

In this example, we changed the text of the error message at each level. In practice, you do not want to have code that has to interpret the text of error messages (especially if the messages have been internationalized). A better approach is to have numeric error codes that can be interrogated and changed at each level, as appropriate.

A common mistake is to not include any code to catch and report unexpected programming errors. Without such code, you are relying on the language runtime library to do this for you. While this may be OK for the typical student program, it is inadequate for a real-world system. The typical runtime libraries often do not provide sufficient debugging information and a real-world system needs to attempt some form of recovery. You need to place code that will catch all possible errors at the following points:

1. All exits from any thread that you create

2. Return to the runtime library from an event handler in your program

3. Exit from the main program

Note that while we probably do not want to report that low-level error message to the user, we do want to record it in our event log for possible future debugging of a problem in the system. If this is a serious error, especially one that causes a server to stop operating, then the system should attempt two things:

1. Send a notification to the appropriate network operations staff. In a large organization, network operations will typically have a network status system that can receive (e-mail) notifications. These notifications will need to conform to the standards set by the network operations staff.

2. Attempt to recover from the error. At a minimum, a server should attempt to restart itself.

4.2 Data Validity

Never assume that data received from the outside world is valid until you have completely verified that it is indeed correct.

One of the most common mistakes that developers make is assuming that data that is received from outside the program is in the expected format. This is often not true simply because of an error on the part of another developer or even just a typing mistake by the user. The result of this assumption is that the program can do wildly unexpected things.

Malicious people (hackers) often take advantage of this assumption. This is the root cause of the infamous Buffer Overflow, SQL Injection, and Cross-Site Scripting attacks. These attacks are often described as exploiting a security problem. However, the problem is really a lack of robustness. Consider Example 4.1, which shows an SQL Injection attack.

```
A program asks the user to enter an account number.

The program assumes the user is doing the expected action and
substitutes what the user enters for the XXX in the following
SQL command:

  SELECT AccountBalance FROM BankAccounts WHERE
  AccountNumber='XXX'

Suppose the user enters this string:

  1004';UPDATE BankAccounts SET AccountBalance='1000000' WHERE
  AccountNumber='2010

Without any Data Validity checking, the user will now have
changed the balance in account 2010 to one million dollars.
```

Example 4.1 *SQL Injection Example*

Whenever data of any kind (including program updates) is received from the user, another computer, or even another process in the same computer, your first step is to verify *syntactic correctness* (i.e., the data is in the correct format). These steps should be taken:

- Verify that the overall length of the data is within expected bounds. A message cannot be too long or too short.
- Verify that the length of each field in the data is within the expected bounds. Again, each field cannot be too long or too short.
- Verify that each field is the correct data type (e.g., numeric, all alphabetic). Check every character of the field to verify that it meets the expected requirements.

Once the syntactic correctness is verified, then you need to verify the *semantic consistency* of the data. This includes:

- Verify that all of the required fields are present.
- Verify that the value in each field is within the expected range.
    - Numeric values cannot be too big or too small.
    - Be very careful before you allow someone to specify the complete pathname for a file. This can have very unexpected results.
- Verify that the values in the various fields are consistent with each other.

Once you have verified the semantic consistency of the data, then you need to verify the *functional correctness*. This requires verifying that the request, including all of its options, is a valid request coming from this client. Understand how the programming language runtime handles various calculation boundaries (e.g., numeric overflow, division by zero, square root of a negative number). Detect these situations and handle them appropriately.

Only after all of these steps have been completed can you safely process the data that was received. Consider Example 4.2. This is an example of an erroneous GiftCard client `Request` message (see Section 3.9). In this example, there are too many digits in the transaction ID, which is a potential buffer overflow problem. The Transaction Type field is empty, which is a potential erroneous execution problem.

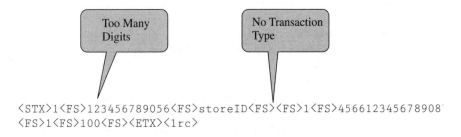

```
<STX>1<FS>123456789056<FS>storeID<FS><FS>1<FS>456612345678908
<FS>1<FS>100<FS><ETX><1rc>
```

Example 4.2   *Gift Card System—Erroneous Request Message*

You can help mitigate a data validity problem by properly designing the communication between components. When one component generates output to other components in the form of structured messages such as queries or requests, it needs to separate the control information and metadata from the actual data. For example, use stored procedures for database access to avoid including actual SQL commands in the data being transmitted.

4.3 System Failures

A *system failure* is any kind of failure that interrupts the normal functioning of the application. Generally, there are the following kinds of system failures:

- *Hardware and Power Failures* Unless the system is running on fault-tolerant hardware, hardware and power failures will stop the application from continuing any kind of execution.

- *Network Failure* A network failure allows the software to continue running but in a restricted manner.

- *Application Failure* An application failure is a severe unexpected error and will cause the termination of the application unless special action is taken.

Student applications can ignore system failures. However, a real-world application must be designed with the knowledge that these things will happen, and more often than one might expect.

> *The network is not reliable.*

As software developers, we tend to think of the network as completely reliable. It is not. Backhoe operators are notorious for breaking communication cables. As the communications companies convert their networks from low-speed analog to high-speed digital, they attempt to save money by reusing the old wiring that was put in place for the analog network. This old wiring tends to have electrical noise on it. That noise had minimal impact on the slow-speed analog connection, but can have catastrophic effects on a high-speed digital connection.

Wireless (Wi-Fi) LANs are also subject to interference. This interference can come from any device using the 2.4 GHz radio frequency. This includes other Wi-Fi devices, as well as wireless telephones, microwave ovens, and Bluetooth devices.

Thus, it is not at all unusual for a network connection to be dropped while an application is executing. Any software system that uses a network connection must comprehend this and the design must explicitly say what actions will be taken in this case. In particular, the design must comprehend that in this situation, you may very likely have the client and server with different state information. How the systems will be returned to a common state is a critical design feature.

Applications will fail when they encounter an unexpected error. If this is a server application, there should be some feature to detect the failure and attempt to restart the server. Otherwise, manual intervention will be required. You do not want to get up at 3:00 AM to restart a server application that failed. You would rather have it restart automatically and then, in the morning, review what caused the failure.

4.4   Transaction Integrity

A *transaction* will compute one or more values and save those values for future use. Thus, a program that simply displays the result of some computations is not executing a transaction. If those results are stored on disk and can be used in a later computation, then it is a transaction. A transaction is partially completed if some but not all of the updated data values have been stored for later use. A system has *transaction integrity* if it can never be left with partially completed transactions.

In a monetary transaction, it is vital that the system be designed to ensure that no party to the transaction loses money because of a system failure. Consider Example 4.3. If a system failure occurs after the subtraction, but before the addition is completed, then the customer will be out $100 and the merchant will not have received his or her money. This is unacceptable.

```
Move $100 from Customer Account to Merchant Account

Steps to Implement
Subtract $100 from Customer Account
Add $100 to Merchant Account
```

Example 4.3   *Transaction Integrity Example*

In nonmonetary systems, the system should be designed to preserve data integrity across a system failure. This *Transaction Integrity* is one of the most important forms of robustness. To ensure Transaction Integrity, the design must ensure that if the transaction is not completed, it appears as though it was never started. In other words, the system must not be left with any partially completed transactions. This can be achieved either through the functioning of the transaction itself or by using a *Journaling System*.

A Journaling System saves sufficient information so that if there is a system failure in the middle of a transaction, upon restart, the system can be returned to a safe state. Typically, this will mean undoing the effects of any partially completed transactions. A relatively straightforward design of a Journaling System is as follows:

1. At the beginning of a transaction, write a `Start_Transaction` record to the journal.
2. Before each resource modification in the transaction, write the state of that resource to the journal.
3. At the end of the transaction, one of two things can be done:
    a. *Commit* the transaction. This accepts all of the changes that have been done and writes an `End_Transaction` record to the journal.
    b. *Rollback* the transaction. The changes are not accepted. The records that have been written to the journal are used to restore the resources to their original state before the transaction began.

Upon restarting after a System Failure, the system will search the journal, looking for incomplete transactions (i.e., those without an `End_Transaction` record). Each incomplete transaction will be rolled back. Figure 4.2 shows an example of the journaling of an incomplete transaction.

In a real system, there are likely to be multiple transactions being processed simultaneously. Thus, the journal will contain records from different transactions all intermixed. To handle this situation, each journal record should have a *transaction identifier*. Then the restart process will use that to match the records for each transaction. See Figure 4.3.

In most real-world systems, the application system will use other software systems such as a database engine. It is important to understand that an application system can provide transaction integrity only if the other software systems that it uses also provide transaction integrity. Thus, the selection of these outside software systems can be critical to the proper functioning of the overall system.

When using a database system, it is critical that Commit and Rollback commands are appropriately used to maintain transaction integrity.

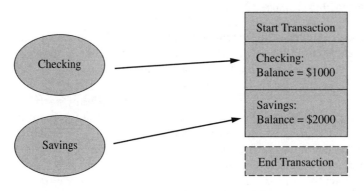

Figure 4.2   *Simple Journaling Example*

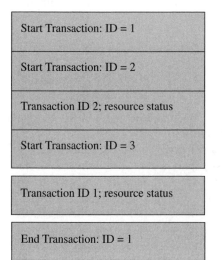

Figure 4.3
Journal with Intermixed Transaction Records

4.5   Java and C# Features

The exception-handling features in Java and C# aid in not only the detection of runtime errors, but also the propagation of them up the call stack, as described in Section 4.1. Whenever an error is detected, an Exception is thrown. You can define your own Exceptions. Having a separate "catch clause" for each type of exception effectively provides an error code for each error. Additionally, since an Exception is defined as a class, you can add your own special processing and error codes to the exceptions that you define. Additionally, the Java compiler forces the developer to either catch each CheckedException or explicitly indicate that it will be propagated up the call tree. This feature helps ensure that you will think about each of these possible errors and what should be done about each one.

Java allows a thread to catch any Exceptions that are not explicitly caught. You can do this by setting an Uncaught Exception Handler for the thread.

JDBC includes support for Commit and Rollback actions. These actions are tied to the Connection object. Thus, if it is possible for a system to simultaneously process multiple transactions, each of those transactions needs to have its own Connection object. This is often accomplished by having a pool of Connection objects that are allocated to each transaction when it begins.

The Java Enterprise Edition (JEE) defines Transaction and TransactionManager Interfaces. JEE defines a functionality framework. Full implementations are available in products such as JBoss and IBM® Websphere. These classes provide support for maintaining transaction integrity.

Similarly, C# has a System.Transaction class that provides support transaction integrity. It is designed to support transactions that are occurring in a distributed environment.

4.6 Case Study

All request messages to the server are encapsulated in a `Request` class, which performs thorough data validity checking.

The GiftCard application has a set of Exception classes that have been defined for it. These Exception classes play a critical role in transforming the error information into something that is relevant to the higher-level context.

The GiftCard server records transactions in a database and uses the Commit and Rollback functions as needed. Similarly, the GiftCard client records transactions in a Transaction Log, which is used at the end of each day to perform the Settlement operation.

If there is a network communications failure, the GiftCard client will report a System Error. When the clerk tries the transaction again, the server will take one of the following actions:

- If the failure occurred while the original request was being transmitted to the server, the server will have no record of it. Consequently, the new transaction will be processed normally.

- If the failure occurred while the response was being transmitted to the client, then the original transaction will be recorded in the server's database. The server will detect the duplicate transaction and return a response with the information from the original transaction (but a message of Duplicate Transaction).

The Application Server (`AppServer`) creates a JDBC Connection object for each transaction processing thread when that thread begins operation. See module SQLDB for details.

4.7 Exercises

1. Describe in detail the data validity testing that the GiftCard server performs on messages received from the client.

2. Suppose a transaction requires several messages back and forth between a client and the server. Describe how database Commit and Rollback functions should be integrated with network failure detection to properly provide transaction integrity.

Design and Programming for Security

> *"We have found the enemy...and it is us"*
>
> —*Pogo*

The fundamental cause of security problems in software is the attitude of developers. We are confident in our own abilities. This leads directly to an attitude that says "My stuff is OK" ... until shown otherwise. On the other hand, an attacker has the attitude that "It's broken...we just need to figure out how." It is important to understand that computer hacking or fraud is no longer the province of some lone person sitting at a computer all day. It has become highly profitable and is now a well-organized international criminal enterprise. If there is a serious profit to be made by breaking into your system, then it will be a target of a highly sophisticated and continuing set of attacks.

There are two primary reasons that your application software will be a target for hackers:

1. The software maintains confidential information (e.g., credit card numbers) that will be valuable to the hacker.

2. The software has system privileges that will be useful to the hacker for further attacks.

5.1 Risk Analysis

To combat this, security must be designed into a system. It requires a thorough analysis of all of the operations of a system and what *can* be done...not just what is expected to be done. This *Risk Analysis* must consider all of the possible attacks and what steps will be taken to mitigate those attacks. Attacks can be mitigated in several ways:

1. The software could be designed to detect and prevent an attack.

2. An operational procedure can prevent an attack from occurring. If this is the recommended solution, be sure that it is well documented and approved by the operations staff.

3. The risk of an attack occurring can be so low or the cost of the attack occurring can be so low as to not justify the cost of explicitly preventing the attack. This will be the business

decision that is made for many types of attacks. However, one must be careful in the analysis of the risk of each attack as one can easily underestimate this.

> *An application that is not robust cannot be secure.*

The single most important thing you can do to ensure the security of your software system is to ensure that the program is robust and thoroughly follow the guidelines in Section 4.2, Data Validity. If one decides to have the software detect and prevent an attack, then one must consider the three areas of Authentication, Authorization, and Secure Communications and Data Storage.

5.2 Authentication

Authentication is the process of verifying that a user or computers are who they say they are. While we are used to a user log on being required by the operating system, applications can also require this process. Similarly, in an environment where not just any arbitrary client can access a server, the server should verify that it is a valid client attempting to communicate with it.

Never have a fixed password in the system for any purpose. This is often included as a mechanism to simpify the job of support people. Unfortunately, this supposed secret code will become known (when, for example, a disgruntled support person quits).

The application log-on process can use almost any of the authentication procedures that the operating system might use, although it is not required that an application use the same procedure as the operating system on that computer. The authentication process can use any combination of:

- *Something You Know* This is the typical password or pin code that everybody is used to. It can also be a picture you recognize or information only you should know (e.g., your first pet's name).

- *Something You Have* This is a physical object that one has, such as a magnetic stripe card (e.g., credit card) or a smart card.

- *Human Features* These are verifiable biometric attributes such as your fingerprint or voiceprint. Facial recognition is not currently accurate enough to be used for user authentication.

Banking systems are now using two-factor authentication; that is, requiring a user to know multiple things. While better than a simple user-ID and password, it is not as strong as requiring both Something You Know and Something You Have. We are already familiar with this mode of operation whenever we use an ATM or debit card, which requires the card and a pin code.

Biometric verification is starting to become more commonplace (laptop computers are available with fingerprint readers).

Many applications require that the client be on one of a specific set of computers. While any or all of these attributes can be used to authenticate a human user, authenticating a remote computer is not quite so simple. The only thing a server has to authenticate a remote system is a stream of bits coming from that computer, which could potentially be faked. There are two approaches to doing this authentication:

- Simply verify a computer-ID number that is included in request messages.

- Use a cryptographic communications protocol between the client and server. Two techniques for doing this are

  - Use *Secure Socket Layer* (SSL) for communications between the client and the server. For common Web communications, SSL is used in a mode in which it only authenticates the server. However, there is another mode in which it can be used to also authenticate the client. SSL requires the parties that are being authenticated to have an X.509 digital certificate to identify themselves. Note that there is significant overhead (and potential cost) to obtain and install these certificates.

  - One can also use the *Kerberos system*, which acts as an Authentication Server for all of the computers in the network.

5.3 Authorization

Once a user or computer is authenticated, then it must be authorized to take certain actions. When designing a software system, always keep the principle of *Least Privilege* in mind. This principle says that a program should only be given the privileges that it actually needs to do its job.

- A program should not have any privilege to any file that it does not actually need to have.

  - *Read Privilege* If a program does not need to read a file, it should not have Read Privilege for it. If a user of a program can use it to read a file that he or she should not have access to, he or she can potentially use it to obtain information for another attack.

  - *Write Privilege* A program should have Write Privilege for a file only if it actually needs to write to it.

  - *Execute Privilege* No data file should ever have Execute Privilege.

  - *Delete Privilege* Just because an application is allowed to write to a file does not mean it should be allowed to delete the file. This is especially important for event logs and database files.

Since the Owner of the various files used by a software system is likely to have all of these privileges, the typical application should always be executed with a different user ID that has limited privileges.

- If a program does not absolutely need *Administrator Privilege* (also known as superuser or root), it should not require it. In fact, administrative privileges are so dangerous and so rarely actually needed, one should separate the code that actually requires administrative privileges into a separate executable. That separate executable should do only the minimum amount that is required with administrative privileges.

- *Application-Level Privileges* also apply. For example, in a typical retail store, a cashier is often not allowed to do voids or refunds. A manager must log on to do those operations. Another example is that certain users are limited as to which fields of a database they can update. The enforcement of Application-Level Privileges should be performed at several levels:

  - The client GUI should nicely disable features that are not available or nicely inform the user that those features cannot be used. This handles the common case of user error.

  - On the other hand, a server must be prepared for the malicious user who is attempting to circumvent the application restrictions. Thus, it must be prepared to do full validation of all requests. This validation needs to be done as an extension of the request validation described in Section 4.2.

Your personal computer isn't.

On Microsoft Windows systems, there are often installation, usability, and security issues because people think of Windows as a single-user system. It is *not*! In almost any corporate environment, the user of a PC will not have administrator rights. Similarly, in a consumer environment, a parent often will give a child Limited User rights. Thus, it will often be the case that the person who installs software is not the person that uses it.

Unfortunately, a large number of commercial applications fail to understand this. The result is a program that violates the security principle of Least Privilege. Examples of such problems include:

- Most programs are started with the Working Directory pointed to the folder that contains the executable. One should always reposition the Working Directory to point to the user's Home Directory. Failure to do this will cause the application to store data files into the Program Files directory.

- The installation process for some programs will install data files into the home directory of the user who is doing the installation. This means that only that user can execute the program.

- Some programs store configuration information into a portion of the Windows Registry that requires administrative privilege to change.

5.4 Secure Data Communications and Storage

The first step in secure data communications and data storage is an analysis of the data that will be communicated and/or stored. This analysis must determine what data truly must be communicated and/or stored. Determine what program data is sensitive. Note that for the continued proper functioning of your program, all program updates will be sensitive. Any sensitive data (such as the contents of a credit card magnetic stripe) for which there is not an absolute requirement to save or transmit, should be deleted as soon as possible. The delete function on most computers simply removes a file system pointer to the data, leaving the contents of the file on the disk. Consequently, the application's delete function for sensitive data should also explicitly erase the data. This erasure should be performed on both disk files and memory areas that may contain the sensitive data.

After performing the analysis described above, if there is still sensitive data that needs to be communicated, it is important that the data communications be encrypted. If any sensitive data will be stored on a mobile system, then it should also be encrypted. One should consider encrypting any sensitive data stored on a nonmobile system as well.

Be sure to use a well-known and secure cryptographic system. Some cryptographic systems require a random number be used as the key. All cryptographic systems function better if the key is randomly selected. A common scheme for creating a key is to have the user enter a pass phrase and then the system computes a hash of that value to be the key. This is essentially the same technique that operating systems use for passwords. Consequently, it is vulnerable to the same type of attacks, such as a dictionary attack.

Since encryption keys rarely need to be manually entered, a better approach is for the system to generate a random value for a key. If you choose to do this, try to avoid using the random number generator that is included with the various programming languages. These random number generators are really *pseudo-random number generators* (PRNG). A PRNG computes the next random number based on the previous value produced. The most common mechanism for doing this is the linear congruent formula:

$$r_i = (ar_{i-1} + c) \bmod M$$

Where a and c are constants and the random number generator produces a value r_i in the range 0 to M.

This predictability of the values is acceptable for the typical uses of random number generators (e.g., probability modeling). However, for cryptographic use, it means that if an attacker can find out one random value, he or she can predict all future random values. This is not acceptable.

In recent years, computers have started to include hardware that will produce a truly random value by sampling the electrical noise on the motherboard. If this feature is available, the cryptographic libraries for that computer will have a random number generator that uses it. Thus, one should use the random number generator in the cryptographic libraries rather than the one that comes with the programming language.

5.5 How Much Information to Report?

Especially when an error occurs, you want to provide sufficient information for the user to understand and be able to correct the error. However, you do not want to provide more than the necessary amount of information. For example, it is not unusual to see an error message that is an exact quote of the error that was reported by a low-level module such as the SQL Engine. The detail in that SQL Engine message is not necessary for the end-user to figure out what he or she needs to do, but it may provide details about the underlying database structure that a hacker can then use to attack the system. This is especially problematic if there is a flaw in the Data Validity testing in the system. The result could be an SQL Injection attack.

5.6 Case Study

Table 5.1 shows the Risk Analysis and corresponding preventive actions for the GiftCard System.

Table 5.1   *GiftCard System Risk Analysis*

Risk	Mitigation
A clerk may sell goods and not charge the card or he or she may add funds to a card and not receive proper payment.	The server limits each card to a maximum of $100. This limits the effect of this potential fraud. Additionally, this is similar to other potential frauds that a retailer could incur. We expect that the store will take similar steps to handle these frauds as it does for its regular sales.
The user could lose his or her card or it could be stolen.	This is the same risk that other anonymous gift cards have. Consideration was given to requiring the user to enter a pin, but that was left as a possible future enhancement if it was felt that it was necessary.
Someone could forge a card.	The server will reject cards with invalid account numbers. If the forgery is on proper card stock and has an already activated account number, the system will accept it. Because of the relatively small limit on the card, this fraud was expected to have a low likelihood. Operational procedures were put in place to handle this situation if it arose.

For various business reasons, only some merchants are allowed to sell or add value to a gift card. A clerk or merchant who is not allowed to do this transaction could attempt it.	A configuration parameter is downloaded to each client system indicating whether GiftCard sales are permitted. If they are not, the client application disables the Add Value button in the GUI. Whenever the server receives an Add Value transaction, it verifies that the database indicates that the sending merchant is permitted to do this operation. *This is an example of never relying on the client to provide security for the server.*
A hacker could impersonate a client system.	The server will reject a terminal with invalid terminal-ID or merchant-ID. Most clients use a dialup connection to the server. The server's dialup communications handler uses caller-ID to validate the location of incoming connections. Two-way authenticated SSL communications was considered for Internet-based clients. However, this was left as a possible future enhancement because of the expense and expected low likelihood of this attack.
A hacker could attempt to directly connect to the database.	Since the server's database is where the money really exists, this was considered a more profitable and therefore more likely attack. The network firewall was configured to disallow incoming connections on port 3306 (the port used by the MySQL database). Thus, only an insider could mount this attack. Only a very limited number of personnel were provided with the user-ID and (randomly chosen strong) password for the database.

5.7   Exercises

1. Describe how requiring a pin code with each transaction could improve security for the GiftCard system. How does requiring a pin complicate deployment of the gift cards?

2. Describe the security issues associated with "who you trust" with access to confidential data.

chapter 6

Using Threads and Processes

Every independent activity can have its own virtual CPU.

A typical modern application system often has many things that could be done at the same time. If one takes advantage of this by using multiple threads or processes in the system, the overall performance and responsiveness of the system can be improved. There are a number of reasons for this:

1. While one thread or process is waiting for an input-output (I/O) request, a separate thread or process can be executing; thus achieving overlap and improving performance.

2. Similarly, while one thread is performing an activity, another thread can be responding to some external event, thus improving responsiveness.

3. On a modern computer, there will often be two or more CPUs that can all be working on different parts of the software system.

6.1 Identifying Required Threads

There are some cases where using separate threads is absolutely required. Many language runtime libraries use a single thread to handle events in the GUI (e.g., mouse click). This thread executes the event listeners in your GUI code. If you use this thread to perform a very time-consuming operation as a result of a GUI event, then while that time-consuming operation is in progress, the system will not be able to react to another GUI event. Thus, your application will seem sluggish. That thread may also be responsible for updating the screen. In that case, your application will behave extremely poorly.

To make matters worse, the runtime libraries often use this same thread to display dialog boxes. Thus, if in your code to handle a GUI event you decide to display a dialog box, the dialog box will not be displayed because the thread that would do that is executing your code. Your program will be "hung."

Similar situations can occur for other event listeners. For example, there is a library called Jpos that provides classes for communicating with point-of-sale devices (in a cash register). The Event Listeners for these library classes behave in a similar manner.

Recommendation: Never do anything that might cause the system's Event Thread(s) to wait. If the code to handle an Event Listener needs to do anything more than update the screen, it should be performed in a separate thread.

6.2 Identifying Opportunities for Parallel Execution

The key to identifying threading opportunities is to find the independent activities within a program. The first kind of independent activity is *Completely Independent Activities*. These activities have absolutely no data in common. Examples include:

- A server can assign a separate thread to handle individual requests arriving from clients.

- In some cases, the processing of a large amount of data can be split up among multiple threads. Section 8.7 discusses this in detail.

It is also possible to use threads for *Relatively Independent Activities*. These activities work mostly independently of each other. However, there is a small amount of well-defined data communication among them. This data communication falls into two categories:

- In the first type, the threads work independently except when they are modifying common data.

- The second type is commonly called a Producer–Consumer scenario. In this situation, one thread (the Producer) creates data to be used by another thread (the Consumer). Section 7.3 explains how this communication works.

The best way to determine what the completely independent and relative independent activities are is to create a Data Flow graph for the system. A *UML Collaboration Diagram* provides this information. Any objects that have zero collaboration with each other (either directly or indirectly) will be candidates to run as separate threads. These objects (or groups of objects) will appear as islands in the collaboration diagram. An object that has a small number of collaborations will also be a candidate if it performs a time-consuming operation or the communication occurs repeatedly. See Figure 6.1.

If object A sends a message to object B and then waits for a response (directly or indirectly) from object B (Figure 6.2), there will usually be no benefit from using separate threads for the two objects. If object A does not wait for the response from object B, then it can be considered as an opportunity to use multiple threads.

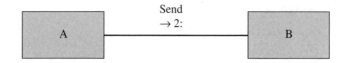

Figure 6.1   *UML Diagram: One-Way Communication*

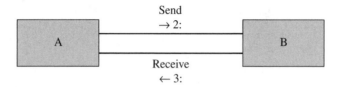

Figure 6.2   *UML Diagram: Two-Way Communication*

Starting with the UML Collaboration Diagram, circle the objects that will be in each thread. This will give you a *Thread Interaction Diagram* (also known as a *Task Diagram*). Every interaction is a place where two threads cannot work independently of each other. Thus, you want to create this diagram so as to minimize the number of interactions among threads while, at the same time, maximizing the opportunity for parallel activity. Figure 6.3 shows a UML Collaboration Diagram. In this system, the GUI will initiate a Transaction, which will record the result of its processing in a `TransactionLog` and use the `PrintManager` to produce a report. The GUI will also start a `Settlement` activity, which will use the data recorded in the `TransactionLog` for its processing and use the `PrintManager` to produce a report.

Figure 6.4 shows a *Task Diagram* that was created from this UML Collaboration Diagram. The `Transaction` and `Settlement` objects execute for considerable time and therefore are in separate threads from the GUI. Similarly, the `PrintManager` executes for a considerable time, but the `Transaction` and `Settlement` objects do not wait for it to complete. Consequently, it is in its own thread. While the `TransactionLog` may execute for considerable time, both the `Transaction` and `Settlement` objects must wait for it to do their processing. Consequently, it is in the same thread as each of those two objects.

There are two general kinds of threads:

- One kind receives an initial message and then proceeds on its own to perform some operation. The thread you would use to process a GUI event would typically be this kind. Similarly, a Web server thread to process a particular browser's request is this type.

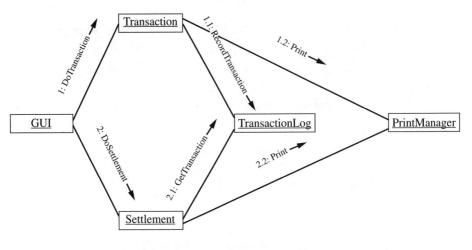

Figure 6.3 *UML Collaboration Diagram*

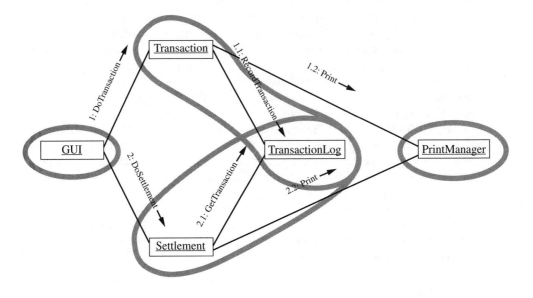

Figure 6.4 *Thread Interaction Diagram*

- The second kind repeatedly receives messages and does appropriate processing for each message. This type of thread is typically implemented as a *Finite State Machine*. A Finite State Machine has:
  - Multiple states
  - Performs a unique function in each state
  - Transitions from one state to another based on an event (message) that is received from outside the finite state machine

By examining the Thread Interaction Diagram, you can see what type of thread each should be.

6.3   Process or Thread?

A Process is the execution of a program. A Thread is an independent execution path with a Process. A Thread uses all of the resources (most importantly, the memory) of the Process that contains it. Consequently, a Thread requires very little system overhead to start, whereas a Process may require significantly more overhead. On the other hand, because a thread uses the same memory as other threads, it has a much greater risk that a problem in one thread will corrupt another.

So, how do we choose whether to implement a parallel activity as a process or a thread?

- If the parallel activity is the execution of an already existing program, it must be done as a separate process.
- If the parallel activity requires use of administrator privileges, then it should be done as a separate process to maintain the principle of Least Privilege (see Section 5.2).
- If the parallel activity may be executed on a different computer, it must be implemented as a separate process.
- If the parallel activity will be rarely executed, it may be desirable to implement it as a separate process.
- If the parallel activity has significant communication with other activities, it will perform better if it is implemented as a Thread in the Process that contains the other activities.

6.4 Thread Encapsulation

One must be very careful when implementing threads. Example 6.1 shows a class (TransactionProcessor) and the usual Java code to start it executing as a separate thread. This is poorly encapsulated because there is usually no need for the code outside a class to know that it runs as a separate thread. In Section 7.4, we shall see that this poorly encapsulated form can easily lead to race conditions.

Example 6.2 shows the same code implemented in a properly encapsulated manner. By placing all of the code for starting the separate thread into the class's constructor, the encapsulated code is neater and easier to understand. In effect, the poorly encapsulated version says that we have an object and, by the way, we are running it as a separate thread. This version says that the object is a thread and that is fundamental to its nature.

Example 6.3 shows an alternate implementation that can be used if the class is a subclass of another class.

```
// Create a transaction processor
TransactionProcessor tp = new TransactionProcessor();

//Run the transaction processor as a separate thread
Thread t = new Thread(tp);
t.start();
```

```
public class TransactionProcessor implements Runnable
{
    // Separate thread begins here
    public void run()
    {
    // Code to be executed in a separate thread
    }
}
```

Example 6.1   *Poorly Encapsulated Threading*

```
// Create a transaction processor
TransactionProcessor tp = new TransactionProcessor();

public class TransactionProcessor extends Thread
{
    // Object's Constructor does thread startup on itself
    public TransactionProcessor()
    {
        // Code to initialize instance variables

        //Run the transaction processor as a separate thread
        //(Should be last step of constructor)
        this.start();
    }

    // Separate thread begins here
    public void run()
    {
        // Code to be executed in a separate thread

    }
}
```

Example 6.2   *Encapsulated Threading*

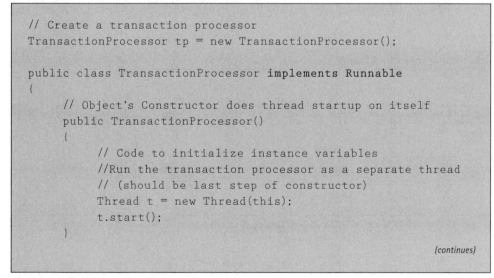

```
// Create a transaction processor
TransactionProcessor tp = new TransactionProcessor();

public class TransactionProcessor implements Runnable
{
    // Object's Constructor does thread startup on itself
    public TransactionProcessor()
    {
        // Code to initialize instance variables
        //Run the transaction processor as a separate thread
        // (should be last step of constructor)
        Thread t = new Thread(this);
        t.start();
    }
```

(continues)

Example 6.3   *Alternate Threaded Object*

```
// Separate thread begins here
public void run()
{
// Code to be executed in a separate thread
}
}
```

Example 6.3 *Alternate Threaded Object* (continued)

6.5 Java and C# Features

Java and C# do not have any syntactic features for creating threads. Instead, both have a built-in class called `Thread`. A class that wishes to create a separately running thread needs to

1. Instantiate a `Thread` object.
2. Call the start method on that `Thread` object.
3. In Java, this will cause a new thread to begin execution at the `run` method in an object you specify. In C#, the new thread will begin execution at a method whose name was passed as a delegate to the `Thread` constructor.

See Examples 6.1 through 6.3 in Section 6.4.

Java includes a facility for starting a separate process. Example 6.4 shows a simple example.

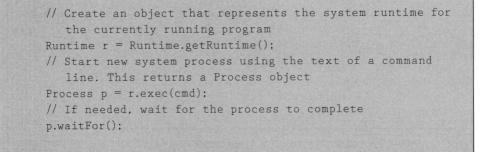

```
// Create an object that represents the system runtime for
   the currently running program
Runtime r = Runtime.getRuntime();
// Start new system process using the text of a command
   line. This returns a Process object
Process p = r.exec(cmd);
// If needed, wait for the process to complete
p.waitFor();
```

Example 6.4 *Java Code to Start a Separate Process*

6.6 Case Study

Following the recommendations in this chapter, the GiftCard client has the following threads:

- GUI Main thread that provides user interface.
- Transaction Processing transactions is time-consuming and is initiated from a GUI event handler. Therefore, it is a separate thread.
- Spooler Printing to a directly connected printer is time-consuming and is a separate thread.

On the server side, the Application Server will create multiple threads to handle the independent requests being received from the various clients.

6.7 Exercises

1. Explain why it is desirable for an object that executes as a separate thread to start the thread itself rather than having it done elsewhere.

2. When you create a Task Diagram, why is it desirable to simultaneously minimize the number of interactions between threads and maximize the opportunities for parallel activity?

3. In the GiftCard client, why is it desirable to run the Spooler as a separate thread? Why shouldn't it be a separate process?

Synchronization and Deadlock Prevention

> *When two processes have a race, you will always be the loser.*

When one is using multiple threads and/or processes, there will often be cases of multiple threads and/or processes needing to access common data. If we blithely allow these threads to modify the common data without any controls, a *race condition* will occur. It is called a race condition because it is indeed a race to see which thread will modify the data first. If they get to the data at the same time, they will incorrectly modify it, thus producing erroneous results. These erroneous results then tend to propagate to other parts of the program.

Whether a race condition will actually cause a problem depends on the timing of the two threads, which in turn, depend on everything else that is going on in that computer. Consequently, these types of problems are rarely discovered during testing. Instead, they remain hidden until the right timing occurs during production usage of the program. These problems are very difficult to find because they leave the system in a totally unexpected state. You will then spend an inordinately large and frustrating amount of time trying to figure out what is happening.

The *dynamic reference complexity C* of an object is

$$C = ort$$

where

o is the number of objects that reference this object
r is the number of objects it references
t is the number of threads that reference this object

Since there can be many instances of each class and many threads referencing an object, the dynamic reference complexity of an object can be much larger than the static reference complexity of the corresponding class. Thus, one can see that resolving race conditions in a poorly encapsulated program can be extremely difficult. This is compounded by the fact, that in most programming languages, there is nothing in the syntax of the program that indicates that multiple threads may be using an object. The complexity of solving this type of problem can quickly grow beyond human comprehension.

7.1 Synchronization Techniques

We want to avoid the types of problems discussed above by making our code *thread-safe*. A module is thread-safe if it uses proper *synchronization* to avoid race conditions. The most commonly used method of synchronization is to use semaphores. A *semaphore* is a software resource with two operations:

- *Lock* and *Unlock* (also known as *Wait* and *Notify*)

You associate a semaphore with each item of common data and then Lock the semaphore before using the data and Unlock it when you are done (see Example 7.1). The functionality of the Lock call is to ensure that this thread is the only one that can proceed to access the common data. Any other thread that attempts to Lock the semaphore while this thread has it locked will be forced to wait. Unlock will allow waiting threads to attempt to Lock the semaphore again.

While semaphores implement the necessary functionality for proper synchronization, they are subject to easy programming errors. This is illustrated in Example 7.2. Semaphores require that an Unlock be present on all exit paths from the module that performed the Lock. It is easy to forget to include these, especially on error paths.

Example 7.3 shows that it is also possible to have too many unlocks, which will cause race conditions to occur.

A more modern approach is to use a *monitor*. Monitors are supported in Java and C#. With support for monitors, the programmer specifies that a block of code is to be executed with a particular resource locked (synchronized). The compiler then ensures that the resource will be locked on entry to the code block and unlocked on all exits from that code block, thus avoiding the possibility of this type of programming error.

To maintain proper encapsulation, all synchronization commands should be in the same module as the resource being locked. If this is not done, then one must examine all references to the resource in all modules to verify that proper synchronization is actually being performed. Sometimes, one wishes to use a library module that is not thread-safe. In this situation, the best solution is to implement a wrapper module that all other modules reference when they want to use the library module. The wrapper then performs proper synchronization to make it thread-safe.

In Example 7.4, the getter and setter for a shared value are locked. However, the increment of the value is performed outside the lock and can thus be subject to a race condition.

A common solution to this problem is to place a lock around the code in the main program (see Example 7.5). However, this is poorly encapsulated and can easily lead to the problems discussed about poorly encapsulated code.

```
Lock semaphore
Modify common data
Unlock semaphore
```

Example 7.1   *Semaphore Usage*

```
public int methodX()
{
    lock (semaphore);

    if (a>b)
    {
        // semaphore is not unlocked on this exit path
        return;
    }
    unlock (semaphore);
}
```

Example 7.2   *Semaphore with Not Enough Unlocks*

```
public int methodY()
{
    lock (semaphore);
    .
    .
    .
    unlock (semaphore)

    if (a>b)
    {

        return;
    }
    // Semaphore is unlocked again
    unlock (semaphore);
}
```

Example 7.3   *Semaphore with Too Many Unlocks*

```
// Main program
    SharedData data = new SharedData();

    data.setValue(data.getValue() + 1);

public class SharedData
{
    private int value;
    public synchronized int getValue()
    {
        return value;
    }
    public synchronized void setValue(int newValue)
    {
        VALUE = NEW VALUE;
    }
}
```

Example 7.4 *Poor Encapsulation Can Lead to Race Conditions*

```
// Main program
    SharedData data = new SharedData();

    Synchronized (data)
    {
        data.setValue( data.getValue() + 1);
    }
```

Example 7.5 *Common Poorly Encapsulated Solution*

Example 7.6 is properly encapsulated with the shared data having an *increment* method that has proper locking and avoids the race condition. Additionally, if there is no need for this shared value to be arbitrarily changed at arbitrary times, the setValue method should be deleted and an `initializeValue` method provided instead. The name of this method should be a clue that it should not be used for setting values at arbitrary times. It would even be possible for the `initializeValue` method to throw an exception if it is called more than once. These types of design features can tremendously reduce the possibility of race conditions or even make them impossible.

```
// Main program
    SharedData data = new SharedData();

    data.increment();

public class SharedData
{
    private int value;
    public int getValue()
    {
        return value;
    }
    public void setValue(int newValue)
    {
        value = new value;
    }
    public synchronized int increment()
    {
        return value++;
    }
}
```

Example 7.6   *Proper Encapsulation*

7.2   Where to Synchronize?

The Task Diagram provides the information we need to determine where synchronization is necessary. The following algorithm identifies the necessary synchronization:

1. Any object that is in more than one thread is actually common data that is being accessed by those threads. All code blocks in such an object should be properly synchronized.

2. All messages (method calls) from one thread to another need to be synchronized.

3. Identify all of the static and instance variables accessed in step 2.

4. All code blocks that access the variables identified in step 3 also need to be synchronized.

Figure 7.1 shows the Task Diagram from Chapter 6. We can clearly see that the messages from the GUI thread to the Transaction and Settlement threads will require synchronization. Similarly, we see that the message from the Transaction and Settlement threads to the PrintManager require synchronization. We can also see that the TransactionLog object is common data shared by the Transaction and Settlement threads. Consequently, all messages to that object will require synchronization. Finally, synchronization will be required on all code blocks that access the same data as the messages we have just discussed.

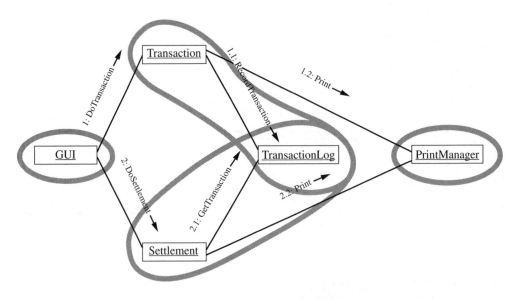

Figure 7.1   *Thread Interaction Diagram*

7.3 Producer–Consumer Scenario

A common situation is for one thread (the Producer) to create data to be used by another thread (the Consumer). The data is transferred from the Producer to the Consumer via a Buffer, which is typically finite in size (see Figure 7.2). This is also commonly called the Bounded Buffer Problem.

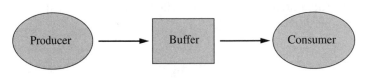

Figure 7.2   *Producer–Consumer*

It is pretty obvious that for this scenario to work, the Consumer must wait if the Buffer is empty. It is not quite as obvious that the Producer must wait if the Buffer is full. An implementation of this Bounded Buffer Problem requires three resources; the Buffer itself; one indicating the Buffer is empty; and another indicating that it is full. See Figure 7.3. Notice that the size of the Buffer acts as a throttle on the Producers. Adjusting the size of the Buffer can dramatically affect the overall performance.

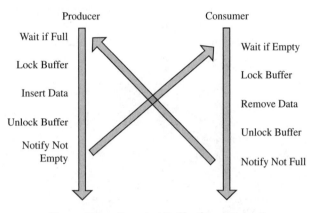

Figure 7.3   *Bounded Buffer Communication*

An optimization of this communication structure is possible if you know that there will only be a few simultaneous accesses to the communications buffer. In that case, you can simply use the underlying memory management system as the throttle on the producer(s). Each producer obtains the memory for the data from the memory management system and then places it onto a linked list that acts as the buffer. The Consumer still has to wait if the Buffer is empty, but the Producers never have to directly wait on the Buffer to be not full (Figure 7.4).

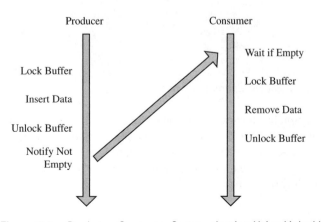

Figure 7.4   *Producer–Consumer Communication Using Linked List*

7.4 Race Conditions in Starting a Thread

Example 7.7 shows the natural temptation on how to start multiple threads executing for a class. Notice that each thread will use the same Object and, therefore, the same instance variables. Thus, you immediately have a race condition. This is a disaster in the making. Even synchronizing every method in the class will not help, as you will get into a situation in which some of the Object's instance variables will have values from one thread and other instance variables will have values from another thread. When this disaster occurs, you will spend a very long time wondering why the instance variables have such strange inconsistent values.

```
// Create a transaction processor
TransactionProcessor tp = new TransactionProcessor();

//Start one thread
Thread t1 = new Thread(tp);
t1.start();

// Start another thread
Thread t2 = new Thread(tp);
t2.start();

public class TransactionProcessor implements Runnable
{
    // instance variables (shared by the multiple threads)

    // Separate thread begins here
    public void run()
    {
    // Code to be executed in a separate thread
    }
}
```

Example 7.7   *Poor Encapsulation Leads to Race Condition*

Example 7.8 shows how encapsulated threading (from Section 6.4) is much simpler than the unencapsulated version. It also automatically avoids the race condition problem of the unencapsulated version because it guarantees that there will be a separate Object and therefore a separate set of instance variables for each thread.

```
// Create one transaction processor
TransactionProcessor tp1 = new TransactionProcessor();

// Create another
TransactionProcessor tp2 = new TransactionProcessor();

public class TransactionProcessor extends Thread
{

    // Object's Constructor does thread startup on itself
    public TransactionProcessor()
    {
        // Code to initialize instance variables

        //Run the transaction processor as a separate thread
        //(Should be last step of constructor)
        this.start();

    }

    // Separate thread begins here
    public void run()
    {
        // Code to be executed in a separate thread
    }
}
```

Example 7.8   *Encapsulated Threading*

7.5 Creating Singletons

A singleton is a class that, by design and intent, never has more than one object instantiated from it. They are commonly used to represent a real-world object for which we know there can only be one. A common approach to instantiating a singleton object is to have a public static variable refer to the object (see Example 7.9). Unfortunately, this approach can have a race condition if another thread refers to the singleton object before it has been created (resulting in a Null Pointer Exception).

A better approach is to encapsulate the creation of the singleton into the class itself. This is shown in Example 7.10. In this approach, a public static method in the class itself does the instantiation and avoids the race condition. Each thread that needs to access the singleton object can safely obtain a reference to it by using this method.

```
// Create singleton object
public static SomeClass someObject;

someObject = new SomeClass();
```

Example 7.9 *Poor Singleton Creation*

```
public class SomeClass
{
    // Reference variable initialized to null to indicate
    // object has not been created yet;
    private static SomeClass someObject = null;

    // Static method determines if object has been instantiated
    // If not, it does it
    public static synchronized SomeClass getSomeObject()
    {
        // See if the singleton was previously instantiated
        if (someObject==null)
        {
            // If not, create the singleton object
            someObject = new someClass();
        }
        // Return reference to singleton
        return someObject;
    }
}
```

Example 7.10 *Thread-Safe Singleton Creation*

7.6   Deadlocks

A deadlock is when multiple threads and/or processes are all waiting for each other to release a resource lock. Typically, no release ever occurs and the system is hung. Like Race Conditions, this type of problem is rarely caught in testing, but will rear its ugly head once you put the system into production.

Four conditions must be present in order for there to be a deadlock:

1. *Exclusive Control* At least one resource must be held in exclusive control by one of the processes in deadlock.

2. *No Preemption* A process cannot be interrupted and forced to release one of the resources it holds.

3. *Hold and Wait* A least one of the waiting processes must be holding one of the resources that another process in waiting on.

4. *Circular Wait* The Resource Graph contains a cycle.

A Resource Graph helps illustrate Deadlock scenarios. In this graph, we will use ovals to represent processes and rectangles to represent resources. An arrow from a resource to a process means that process is holding the resource. An arrow from a process to a resource means the process is waiting on the resource. Now consider Example 7.11, which will deadlock. Figure 7.5 illustrates the circular wait that this example exhibits.

Process 1	Process 2
Lock Resource A	Lock Resource B
Lock Resource B	Lock Resource A
Modify Data	Modify Data
Unlock Resource B	Unlock Resource A
Unlock Resource A	Unlock Resource B

Example 7.11   *Deadlock Example*

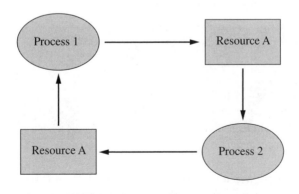

Figure 7.5   *Resource Graph with Deadlock*

7.7   Deadlock Prevention

The key to preventing deadlock is a proper analysis of the system's resource usage. The most effective way to prevent deadlock is to determine whether it is actually necessary to lock more than one resource at a time. If the resources can be updated independently of each other, then each resource can be locked individually rather than all together.

Consider Example 7.12. At first glance, one might think that both accounts need to be locked together to correctly execute these transactions. While each process must update both accounts to maintain transaction integrity, each process can independently update each account (under lock). Independent updating of each account is possible because the addition operation being performed on each account depends only on that account and a constant. Consequently, it is only necessary that each process lock one account at a time while it is being updated. There is no need to lock both accounts together.

```
Process 1 is performing the command:
Move $100 from Jones Family Savings to Jones Family Checking

Process 2 is performing the command:
Move $200 from Jones Family Checking to Jones Family Savings
```

Example 7.12   *Independent Updating*

In Example 7.13, the update for each account is dependent on the value in the other account. Consequently, both accounts must be locked together for the operations to be performed correctly.

```
Process 1 is performing the command:
Swap amounts in Jones Family Savings and Jones Family Checking

Process 2 is performing the command:
Swap amounts in Jones Family Checking and Jones Family Savings
```

Example 7.13   *Dependent Updating*

If there are multiple "resources" that cannot be updated independently, and it is always the case that all of the resources are updated together, then one only needs one lock for the collection of resources. Individual locks are required for each of the resources only if some of the resources are sometimes updated without updating the entire set of resources. It is necessary to lock more than one resource at a time only if the multiple resources cannot be updated independently.

If multiple resources do need to be locked together, then there are two approaches to preventing deadlock.

One can attempt to lock all of the necessary resources at the beginning. If any of the resources cannot be locked immediately, then release all of the resources that have been locked and try again later. This procedure prevents the Hold and Wait condition, but it is problematic:

- In more complicated applications, you do not always know ahead of time exactly what resources will be required.

- It is not always easy to implement since the synchronizing primitives used will typically wait until the resource is available, rather than informing the application that it is unavailable.

The other technique is to be sure that all processes lock the resources in the same order. This will eliminate the Circular Wait condition. To properly implement this technique, the application must use *absolute resource ordering* for the resources rather than *relative resource ordering.*

Relative ordering determines an order for the locks based on the command or transaction being processed. This can lead to deadlock as two processes could lock the resources in different orders.

With absolute ordering, one must plan for some ordering scheme that is external to the commands being processed. For example, one could use the account numbers as the ordering mechanism for bank accounts.

7.8   OS and Database Features

Operating systems will generally provide semaphores for synchronization operations. Typically, the OS will provide *wait* and *notify* system calls to manipulate the semaphore. They provide no support for preventing deadlocks. That is strictly an application-level design problem. Both Microsoft Windows and Linux follow this model.

Most database engines provide Commit and Rollback functions to support transaction integrity. They also support record locking with two different approaches:

- *Pessimistic Concurrency* You lock a record when you first select it and you are guaranteed that no one else can modify it until after you unlock it. Typically, you indicate that you want this to happen when you establish the connection to the database.

- *Optimistic Concurrency* You do not lock each record. Instead, you assume that no one else will modify the record and then check for data consistency when you attempt to update it. This approach can improve performance, as record locking does consume considerable database resources. There are a number of strategies for implementing optimistic concurrency. The simplest is to check a time stamp that is recorded in each record. When you are ready to update, you read the time stamp again and if it does not match, then someone else has updated the record. It is very easy to implement optimistic concurrency incorrectly and have a resulting race condition. As with all race conditions, it will be very difficult to find this kind of problem. Consequently, you should use this strategy only if you are using a library that supports it. An example is Microsoft's Active Data Objects (ADO.NET).

7.9 Java and C# Features

Java includes a syntax feature to support locking objects. You can put the keyword *synchronized* on a code block or a method. In Example 7.14, the specified object is locked while the code block is executing. In Example 7.15, the object that is executing the method is locked while the method executes.

```
public void methodX() {
    synchronized (object) {
    // object is locked while executing this code block


    }
}
```

Example 7.14   *Synchronized Block in Java*

```
public synchronized void methodY() {
// the object (this) that is executing methodY is locked while
    this method is executing

}
```

Example 7.15   *Synchronized Method in Java*

The first form appears to be more general. However, its use can easily lead to poorly encapsulated code. There could be references to "object" scattered all over the program and each of them needs to be examined to determine whether proper synchronization has been used. If you use only the second approach, then you can be assured that you only need to examine that single class to verify that proper synchronization is being performed on all accesses to shared data.

Note that there may be a temptation to use the first form if one needs to lock a resource that is provided by a library module. A better approach is to create a wrapper class with proper synchronization around the library module and have all references to the library class actually refer to the wrapper class.

There will be some situations where the first form is desirable. Proper encapsulation can be guaranteed if these rules are followed:

1. The object being used in the lock is instantiated in the class where the lock occurs.

2. The reference variable for that object is private to that same class (it should be in any case).

3. The object is never passed as a parameter to any other class or returned as the result of a method call into this class.

If the sole purpose of the synchronization is to control access to shared data, then using the synchronized keyword is sufficient. However, if you need to implement producer–consumer communication between threads, then you also need to use the wait and notify methods. Consider Example 7.16. The Buffer class provides the communication between two threads. The Producer calls the put method to store data. It uses the notify method to let the Consumer know that data is available. The Consumer uses the get method, which use the wait method to await the Producer putting data into the Buffer.

```
Public class Buffer {

    public synchronized void put(Object data) {
        // Place data into data storage area
        notify();  // Notify consumer that data is available
    }

    public synchronized Objet get() {
        wait();     // Wait for data from Producer
        return item from data storage area
    }
}
```

Example 7.16 *Use of Wait and Notify*

C# provides very similar synchronization features with the major exception that the second form of synchronization (where one specifies locking on a method) is not available. Example 7.17 shows the C# syntax. This lack of the second form of synchronization is unfortunate as it makes it very easy to create poorly encapsulated programs. If you are using C#, be sure to follow the rules above for ensuring proper encapsulation.

```
public void methodX() {
    lock (object) {
    // object is locked while executing this code block


    }
}
```

Example 7.17 *Synchronized Block in C#*

Java has no built-in feature for locking a resource across multiple processes. You would need to create a Native Interface to a routine that accesses an underlying operating system feature. On the other hand, C# supports the .NET class called Mutex that provides access to a resource lock provided by the Windows operating system.

In C#, you can use the .NET class ReadWriteLockSlim to control access to a resource by multiple readers and writers. This provides the same type of functionality as Java's wait and notify method calls.

7.10 Case Study

The Util package contains a class called EventQueue. This class implements the Linked List approach for producer–consumer communication. It is used extensively by the Comm communications package.

The GiftCard client uses synchronized methods to protect access to common data (in the TransactionLog class) and for producer-consumer communication in the Spooler class.

7.11 Exercises

1. Explain how the Task Diagram shows where synchronization is required.
2. Examine the EventQueue class in the GiftCard program's Util class. Is this an example of shared data? Explain.
3. Explain the difference between Independent Updating and Dependent Updating of shared data.

chapter 8

Performance Improvement

> *A properly focused effort in performance improvement can have a significant impact.*

There are a number of techniques that can be used to improve the performance of a software system. Unfortunately, there is a tendency to spend time on things that will not have a significant impact and are therefore a wasted effort.

8.1 Algorithm Selection

If the program must work with multiple data items (e.g., search a list of names), then the selection of an algorithm will be critical to the performance of the system. In such a system, we measure the performance of an algorithm relative to n, the number of data items. See Table 8.1. While one might be able to speed up the processing of each data item, for large values of n (the number of data items), the choice of algorithm will have a much larger impact. Thus, if at all possible, one should attempt to use algorithms that have $O(k)$ (i.e., constant) or $O(\log_2 n)$ performance and *absolutely avoid* algorithms that have an $O(n^2)$ performance measure.

Table 8.1   *Algorithm Scalability*

Performance	Scalability	Number of Operations $n = 1000$	$n = 1{,}000{,}000$
$O(k)$	Excellent	1	1
$O(\log_2 n)$	Excellent	10	20
$O(n)$	Good	1000	1,000,000
$O(n\log_2 n)$	Good	10,000	20,000,000
$O(n^2)$	Poor	1,000,000	1,000,000,000,000

It is important to understand the performance of each algorithm being selected and relatively how often that algorithm will be used. Suppose the program must periodically insert information in a table that will be searched later. There will be one performance measure for the insertion algorithm and one for the search algorithm. If the insertions will be done infrequently, then a slower algorithm for it may be acceptable as long as a fast algorithm is used for the searches.

One of the most common operations that an application will do is to search a set of data for a particular item. There are three common search algorithms:

- *Linear Search* This algorithm simply starts at the beginning of a list and scans sequentially through the list until it finds the desired item. Its performance is $O(n)$. More precisely, on average, one will need to search half of the list to find the desired item. Since this search algorithm works with unsorted lists, there is little overhead to create the list.

- A *Hash Table* uses a hash function to distribute the items across the hash table. A Hash Function takes a potentially arbitrary length value and computes a value that fits into a smaller range. After computing the hash function, this system typically uses a linear search to find the desired item from among those that have the same hash value. As long as the hash function uniformly distributes items across the range of the table, this mechanism effectively acts as a linear search whose search length is divided by t, the size of the table. However, if the hash function clusters many items together, it will have minimal improvement over the linear search.

- *Binary Search* This algorithm requires a sorted list, but will find the desired item very quickly as it has a performance of $O(\log_2 n)$. Since a sorted list is required, this algorithm incurs the additional overhead of creating that sorted list. If the list is already sorted for other reasons, then this is an excellent choice. If the list needs to be created in a sorted fashion, then a common approach is to use a *Binary Tree*. This structure organizes the data into a tree and uses a Binary Search to find where to insert a new item into the sorted list.

8.2 Disk I/O

> *The most efficient disk I/O request is one that is never requested!*

When a program is running slowly, the typical approach is to see whether one can optimize the code (CPU instructions). Unfortunately, for most programs, this will have minimal impact. While there are certainly some programs in which the performance bottleneck is the CPU, the vast majority of real-world programs do a significant amount of I/O. Now consider that on a modern computer, a

CPU instruction can be executed in under 1 nanosecond whereas a disk access (seek time + rotational latency) will on average take 10 milliseconds. Thus, one can execute 10 million instructions in the time it takes do one disk access. So which is going to be easier: eliminating 10 million instructions or eliminating one disk I/O?

Disk I/O requests will often be hidden in other software such as a database engine. In Example 8.1, the database engine needs to read through the Customers table twice. In Example 8.2, the database engine only needs to read the table once. Messages sent across the Internet to another system will often result in that system performing one or more disk I/O requests.

```
Select Name from Customers
Select Address from Customers
```

Example 8.1 *Inefficient Database Access*

```
Select Name, Address from Customers
```

Example 8.2 *Efficient Database Access*

8.3 Buffering

This will reduce the amount of physical I/O requests by the buffering factor used. For example, if we buffer three logical I/O requests per physical I/O request, the number of physical I/O requests will be one-third the number required without buffering. We do this by having the application's logical I/O requests copy data to and from a large memory buffer. The physical I/O requests then transfer the entire buffer. As an example, an application may wish to do a logical I/O request for each line of a text file. We can increase system performance by doing only one physical I/O request for a large group of lines.

If you can't completely eliminate I/O, make the physical I/O requests as big as possible.

Example 8.3 illustrates a general algorithm that is used for buffered writes (see Figure 8.1).

Figure 8.2 illustrates a Buffered Read, which would use the algorithm in Example 8.4.

Notice that with Buffered Writes, we are keeping data in volatile memory for a longer period before we physically write it to nonvolatile memory. Thus, we are incurring a greater risk that we will lose data if there is a system crash. Our

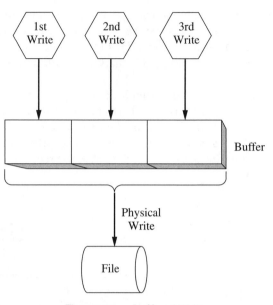

Figure 8.1   *Buffered Write*

```
Copy application data to buffer[Buffer_index]
Buffer_index = Buffer_index + logical_write_size
If Buffer_Index = Buffer_Size  // is Buffer now Full?
    Do physical write
    Buffer_index = 0
```

Example 8.3   *Buffered Write Algorithm*

overall application and system design should understand and handle this. In any case, we must *close* the file when we are done writing to it. The close operation will ensure that all data has been written from the buffer to the I/O device.

If the data we are buffering is for a transaction, we *must* transfer the data to nonvolatile memory when the transaction completes. Otherwise, we cannot ensure transaction integrity. For ordinary file I/O, the *Flush* system call is used to do this. Flush effectively says to ignore the buffering and do a physical write immediately. If one is using a database engine, the *Commit* command is used for this purpose.

Buffering is an example of a *Space–Time Tradeoff*. By using more memory space, we can potentially save time. For pure Buffering, it is easy to calculate:

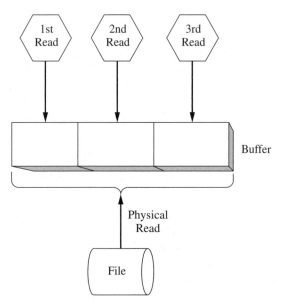

Figure 8.2 *Buffered Read*

```
If Buffer_index == Buffer_Size   // Have we emptied the buffer?
    Do physical read
    Buffer_index = 0
Copy data from buffer[Buffer_index] to application
Buffer_index = Buffer_index + logical_read_size
```

Example 8.4 *Buffered Read Algorithm*

- The Benefit (time saved)

$$T = D\left(\frac{B}{l} - 1\right)$$

where
   D is the Disk Access Time
   B is the Buffer Size
   l is the logical read size

- The Cost (extra memory space required)

$$C = B - l$$

8.4 Caching

When you use Buffering, data goes into the Buffer and then is used once and removed from the Buffer. With Caching, data goes into the Cache and then is used potentially multiple times and is not removed from the Cache unless its memory space is needed for something else. There are three critical design issues for a Cache:

- How big to make the cache
- How to organize the data in the cache
- What algorithm to use to select items to be removed from the cache when it is full

One would like a cache to be large enough that it significantly reduces the number of disk I/O operations required. The Hit Ratio is the percentage of data requests that can be found in the cache without doing a disk I/O. If one assumes that all data items are equally probable to be requested in the future, then the Hit Ratio H is

$$H = \frac{M}{k} \cdot M \leq k$$

where M is the size of the cache and k is the number of data elements.

Thus, the larger the cache, the better the performance. Of course, there is no benefit to having a cache that is larger than the number of data elements. However, because the amount of memory is limited, you cannot always make the cache as large as you would like. Thus, we have a space–time tradeoff. In fact, there are a couple of simple guidelines:

- For randomly accessed data, if a 1 KB record will be accessed again within 5 minutes, then the performance improvement of caching the data will justify the additional cost of the memory to hold the data. Conversely, if the data will not be accessed again within 5 minutes, it should not be cached. For a 100-byte record, caching is appropriate if the record will be accessed again within 1 hour.
- For sequentially accessed data, the data should be accessed again within 1 minute to justify caching.

The simplest way to organize the data in the cache is as an array (see Example 8.5). Then you can use an integer index that can be calculated from a loop index.

This approach works very well if every data element in the cache needs to be accessed equally. However, consider a sparse matrix such as in Example 8.6.

| 3.6 | 5.0 | 10.5 | 7.6 | 1.3 | 4.3 | 6.7 | 3.2 |

Example 8.5 *Data Array Cache*

With a sparse matrix, you are not typically accessing every element equally. In fact, the unpopulated elements will be accessed much less than the more densely populated portions of the matrix. Thus, if you use a simple array for a sparse matrix, you will be wasting a large amount of space. In this situation, it might be better to store only the populated data values and have a separate keyed index table to reference the values. Of course, you now need a search algorithm to locate the key in the keyed index table. See Example 8.7.

The third part of a cache design is how to decide which data item to replace if the cache becomes full and a new data item needs to be inserted. This will be very application dependent. A generally effective method is to use a Least Recently Used replacement algorithm. In this algorithm, the software keeps track of which data item was least recently used and chooses it for replacement. This is based on the heuristic that the data item that was most recently used, is also most likely to be used again in the near future. That is not always true, but it works in many situations.

					3.6	5.0	10.5	7.6	1.3
						4.3	6.7	3.2	

Example 8.6 *Sparse Matrix*

Key Table (row, column numbers from sparse matrix)

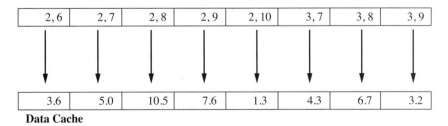

2, 6	2, 7	2, 8	2, 9	2, 10	3, 7	3, 8	3, 9
3.6	5.0	10.5	7.6	1.3	4.3	6.7	3.2

Data Cache

Example 8.7 *Key Table for Sparse Matrix*

Key Table (row, column numbers from sparse matrix)

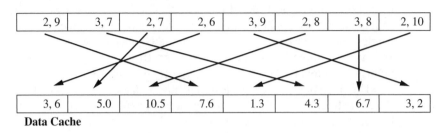

| 2, 9 | 3, 7 | 2, 7 | 2, 6 | 3, 9 | 2, 8 | 3, 8 | 2, 10 |

| 3, 6 | 5.0 | 10.5 | 7.6 | 1.3 | 4.3 | 6.7 | 3, 2 |

Data Cache

Example 8.8   *Key Table Sorted by Recent Use*

A technique for implementing this is to keep the key table sorted by how recently a data item was used. Whenever a data item is used, we move its key table entry to the beginning of the key table. Over time, this will cause the least recently used data item to be at the end of the key table. In Example 8.8, item (2, 9) is the most recently used and item (2,10) is the least recently used. If we need to replace a data item, it will be (2,10). This technique requires a linear search of the key table because it is not sorted by the key values.

Another approach is for the entries in the key table to have a field that has an "access number." The system keeps a counter that is incremented every time a data item is accessed. That counter value is stored into the "access number" field in the key table. When a data item needs to be replaced, the system does a linear search through the key table to find the entry with the smallest access number. That is the least recently used item and can be replaced. If this system is used in conjunction with a Binary Search for normal data accesses (perhaps using a Binary Tree), it can be very efficient.

8.5 Pipes

A *Pipe* incorporates the concept that when a program reads data, that data will come from another program rather than a file. Thus, a pipe has a program at one end that is writing to the pipe and another program reading data at the other end of the pipe (see Figure 8.3). It is often the situation that one program will produce output that another program needs for input. Rather than having the first program write to a file and the second program read that file, we can save time by having each program communicate via a pipe. Using a pipe can improve system performance in two ways:

1. By not using a file, the applications save time by not using a disk I/O.

2. A pipe has the characteristic that the receiving program can read whatever data has already been written. Thus, we do not need to wait until the first

program has written all of the data before we start executing the second program. This creates a pipeline similar to an automobile assembly line to speed up overall performance.

A Pipe will typically use a buffer in main memory as a temporary holding spot for the data that has been written by the first program. Notice that a Pipe is actually an implementation of the Producer–Consumer communication scenario that was discussed in Section 7.3.

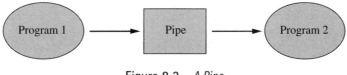

Figure 8.3   *A Pipe*

8.6   Queuing Effects

Especially on server applications, where many requests are being handled simultaneously, not only is each I/O slow, but also a queuing effect can cause each request to wait a very long time while other requests are handled. This can have a truly dramatic effect on the ability of a server application to scale up to handle a large number of simultaneous requests.

Let's consider a simple example. A server receives requests from a client and issues an I/O request as part of creating its response to the client request (see Figure 8.4).

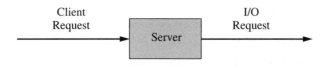

Figure 8.4   *Request Processing*

As shown in Table 8.2, a server that receives a single request can process that request in 10 milliseconds (MS). However, if that same server receives 10 simultaneous requests, the last one processed will take 100 MS, which starts being noticeable. If that server receives 100 simultaneous requests, the last one processed will take a full second. If that server receives 1000 simultaneous requests, the last one processed will take 10 seconds!

Thus, eliminating that one I/O operation for each request will allow this particular server application to scale up to support many more users than it otherwise could. Obviously, we cannot eliminate all I/O operations, but this simple example shows how much eliminating I/O operations can help improve performance.

Table 8.2   *Sample Disk Request Times*

Request	Wait Time (MS)	I/O Time (MS)	Total Request Time (MS)
1	0	10	10
2	10	10	20
3	20	10	30
4	30	10	40
5	40	10	50
6	50	10	60
7	60	10	70
8	70	10	80
9	80	10	90
10	90	10	100

This queuing effect occurs on not only disk I/O requests, but also anytime the processes need exclusive access to a resource. Using a resource goes through several stages, as shown in Figure 8.5.

Figure 8.5   *Stages of a Resource Request*

1. When a request arrives, it goes into a queue to wait for the resource.
2. Once the resource becomes available, there is a resource-specific procedure to obtain access to the resource.
3. After the resource is obtained, it can actually be used.
4. Finally, the resource is released when the request has been completed.

The *Total Request Time* of the *n*th request is the sum of the *Request Wait Time* and the *Request Service Time*.

$$T_n = W_n + S_n$$

The *Request Service Time* for a resource is the sum of the time to obtain the Resource and the time to use the Resource. As we can see from the above example, if we have *n* simultaneous requests for a resource, the *Request Wait Time* for request *n* is the sum of the service times for all of the previous requests:

$$W_n = \sum_{i}^{n-1} S_i$$

where S_i is the Service Time for the i_n request.

To minimize the queuing effect, we should do as little as possible while a resource is locked. The system should be designed so that any time-consuming work is done outside the resource lock.

In the producer–consumer case, only the actual work for the producer to pass the data to the consumer and for the consumer to actually obtain the data should be done under lock. Example 8.9 shows the wrong way to do this. Example 8.10 shows the correct way.

Producer	Consumer
Lock resource	Lock resource
Do lots of work to create the data	Retrieve data from buffer
Place the data into buffer	*Do lots of work with the data*
Unlock resource	Unlock resource

Example 8.9   *Unoptimized Locking*

Producer	Consumer
Do lots of work to create the data	Lock resource
Lock resource	Retrieve data from buffer
Place the data into buffer	Unlock resource
Unlock resource	*Do lots of work with the data*

Example 8.10   *Optimized Locking*

8.7   Parallel Processing

Figure 8.6 shows a typical modern computer, which is a multiprocessor in which all the CPUs share the main memory of the computer. On a computer like this, one can break a problem up into multiple threads or multiple processes. How much performance improvement is achieved depends on how well the program is divided into threads. One should use a thread-profiling tool to see the resulting performance improvement.

> *Modern computers have two or more CPUs.*

Figure 8.7 shows a Cluster System in which multiple computers are connected via a high-speed interconnect system. These computers do not share the same

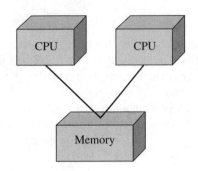

Figure 8.6 *Multiprocessor System*

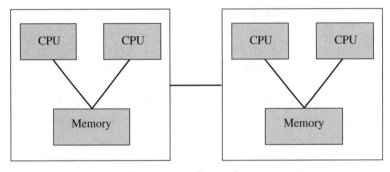

Figure 8.7 *Cluster System*

memory. Consequently, it is not possible to have one process with some threads running on one computer and other threads running on another computer. To take full advantage of this type of system, one must have separate processes available to run on each computer.

With the availability of these types of computer systems, if you need to work on a very large data set, you should consider breaking the data into multiple groups, with each group being handled by a separate thread or process. If you break up the work on a large data set among k threads or processes, you will get almost a factor of k performance improvement as long as

$$k \leq C \leq 8$$

where C is the number of CPUs on the system.

This is possible only if the operations being performed on the data are independent of each other. The operations are independent of each other if no result from any of the operations is used as the input to any other operation. Mathematically, this can be expressed as

$$\forall r_i, r_i \notin D$$

where

D is the set of input data, and

r_i is the result of the i_{th} operation.

In Example 8.11, each operation depends on the result of another operation on the data array. Thus, these calculations cannot be divided up into groups for multiple threads to perform.

In Example 8.12, each operation is independent of the result of any other operation. This operation can be divided into multiple threads.

If you have a situation where the operations are dependent, it may be possible to use a different algorithm in which the operations are independent. Examples 8.11 and 8.12 produce exactly the same results and are therefore equivalent. Thus, the dependent version could be changed to the independent version so that it can be divided up among multiple threads.

```
x[0] = 0;
for (int i=1; i<n; i++)
{
    x[i] = x[i-1] + 1
}
```

Example 8.11   *Dependent Array Operations*

```
for (int i=0; i<n; i++)
{
    x[i] = i
}
```

Example 8.12   *Independent Array Operations*

Example 8.13 shows the independent version of this example broken into multiple threads.

The typical operating system will schedule threads and processes for a multiprocessor system in a manner that will keep all of the processors approximately equally busy. However, current operating systems do not typically have any capability to schedule processes among the computers in a Cluster System. That has to be done by a load-balancing application.

A Cluster System works best when there are many independent requests to be processed simultaneously. Large Websites such as amazon.com and ebay.

```
for (int i=0; i<k; i++)
{

     // Start separate threads, with each one processing a sub-array
     // that is 1/k of the original array
     DivideAndConquer d = new DivideAndConquer(i*n/k, (i+1)*n/k -1);
}


public class DivideAndConquer extends Thread
{
     private int start;
     private int end;

     // Starting and ending array indices are passed in
     public DivideAndConquer(int start; int end)
     {
          this.start = start;
          this.end = end;

     }
     public void run()
     {
          // Work on the sub-array we have been assigned
          for (int i=start; i<end; i++)
          {
               x[i] = i
          }

     }
}
```

Example 8.13   *Multiple Threads*

com are good examples. In this type of system, user requests are first routed to a load-balancing application, which then sends them to one of the computers in a cluster.

Figure 8.8 illustrates the operation of a load-balancing system. In this type of system, while the result of the user request will go directly back to the user, each computer in the cluster will need to report back to the load-balancing system that it has completed a request.

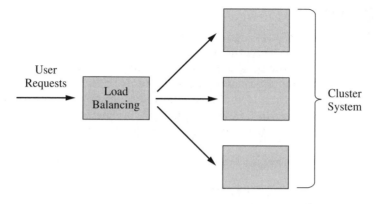

Figure 8.8   *Cluster System Load Balancing*

8.8   Virtual Memory

Virtual Memory is a nice feature provided by the operating system to allow a program to run without the entire program being loaded into memory. This allows us to

- Run more programs at the same time
- Run programs that are bigger than the actual physical memory

While these are useful features, the presence of Virtual Memory can lull us into a false sense that we do not have to be concerned with the amount of memory that is available. The simple way to work with a large amount of data is to have one very large array of the data. Unfortunately, that array can be so large that the operating system starts doing page swapping, which are very time-consuming disk I/O operations. The page-swapping algorithm used by the OS is intelligent, but it does not know as much about how the data is being processed as we do.

In this type of situation, it may be better to divide the data into smaller groups and only load one group at a time into memory for processing. This can avoid unnecessary page swapping and improve the overall performance of the system.

While Virtual Memory is usually available on general-purpose computers, it is often not available on other types of systems. For example, any device without a hard disk (such as a cell phone) is unlikely to have Virtual Memory. On this type of system, it is critical that the application design be cognizant of the available memory.

8.9 Profiling

A *Profiler* is a tool that will instrument and monitor a program and then report on where the program is spending its time. This can be very useful if you are working on a poorly documented or poorly designed program. It can also be useful even if you have followed all of the best practices for designing a program. It can find things that have simply been overlooked. For example, a Profiler can often find places where the program is using an excessive amount of memory.

8.10 Java and C# Features

Java has what are known as the Collection classes for organizing data:

- The `List` classes (`ArrayList` and `LinkedList`) have an implied ordering of the data elements. Consequently, they are best used with a Linear Search.
- The `HashSet` and `HashMap` classes use a Hash Table for the base organization of the data elements.
- The `TreeSet` and `TreeMap` classes use a Binary Tree to organize the data. They provide a "get" method that uses a binary search to locate the desired data element.

A JDBC Connection object uses a significant amount of system resources. This is especially true if the database server resides across the Internet. Consequently, the number of Connection objects that are created should be explicitly limited. Typically, one will create a pool of Connection objects, which are allocated for use as needed.

C# also has a set of Collection classes:

- The `List` classes (`ArrayList`, `List`, and `LinkedList`) have an implied ordering of the data elements. Consequently, they are best used with a Linear Search.
- The `HashSet` and `Dictionary` classes use a Hash Table for the base organization of the data elements.
- The `SortedList` and `SortedDictionary` classes use a Binary Tree to organize the data. They provide a "get" method that uses a binary search to locate the desired data element.

8.11 Case Study

The GiftCard client keeps a cache of its Transaction Log to reduce the amount of disk I/O required. The Spooler module handles printing receipts. Since printing to a directly connected receipt printer is a very time-consuming operation, it is implemented as a separate thread to provide concurrent printing and communication with the GiftCard Server.

8.12 Exercises

1. Explain how the Queuing Effect can cause large delays when processing many requests.
2. Why does disk I/O have such a large impact on performance?

Program Correctness and Testing

> *Most of the bugs in your code will be in the parts we don't test.*

We want the programs we create to work correctly and we naturally approach the problem with confidence in our own capabilities. This naturally leads to the assumption that we have done our own work correctly. So, when a problem is encountered, "It must be caused by a problem somewhere else." This then leads to the common complaint, "There must be a bug in the system libraries." *Wrong!* The bug is probably in your code. We need to approach the task in a less egotistical manner.

> *Testing only finds the next bug.*

If one does thorough testing of an application and finds no bugs, it indicates that the program has the potential to be robust, but it cannot ensure it. This is a critical distinction. If the right design decisions have not been made, then no amount of testing can produce a robust and secure program.

With a properly encapsulated program, the following rule applies:

- A module correctly implements its defined functionality if its code is correct and the code of the classes it references is correct.

Thus, we can perform a simple iterative scan of the modules in a program to determine whether the program is correct. Of course, that simple code inspection will not always find all errors (we are human after all). When we look at our own code, we tend to skip over errors. This is why another person should always perform a *code inspection*.

9.1 Using the Dependency Graph

Testing and Code Inspection both need to use a *Dependency Graph*. A Dependency Graph shows which modules (classes) each module depends on. You can use the following simple algorithm to construct a Dependency Graph:

1. Begin with the UML Class Diagram (such as the one in Figure 9.1).

2. Wherever there is a "uses" relationship, change the line to an arrow pointing in the "uses" direction.

At first glance, this new graph (see Figure 9.2) would seem to show all of the module dependencies. However, let's take a closer look. The Transaction class uses TransactionLog, so Transaction depends on TransactionLog. However, when Transaction calls TransactionLog, one of the parameters that it passes is the current instance of itself. Thus, TransactionLog is also dependent on Transaction. This creates a cycle in the Dependency Graph (see Figure 9.3).

In general, if module A passes an instance of itself to module B, the Dependency Graph will now have a cycle. If module B passes the instance of A to module C, the cycle is enlarged (see Figure 9.4).

Note that when the actual argument passed from A to B is an instance of A, if the formal parameter in B is either an Interface or a base class that A extends, then there is no cycle created in the dependency graph (see Example 9.1).

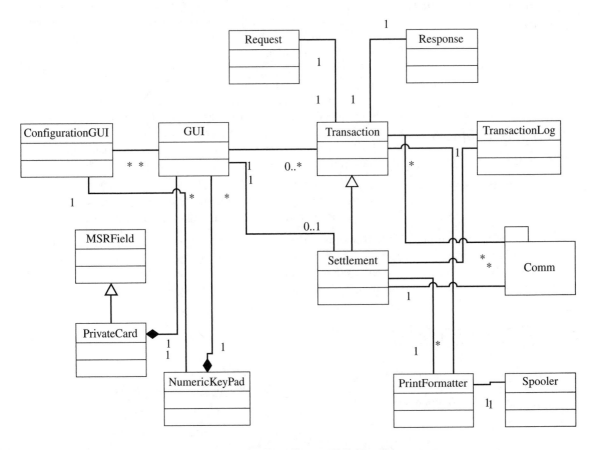

Figure 9.1   UML Class Diagram

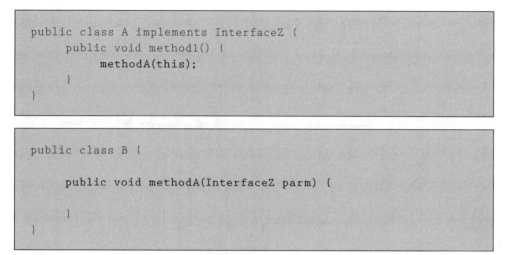

```
public class A implements InterfaceZ {
    public void method1() {
        methodA(this);
    }
}
```

```
public class B {

    public void methodA(InterfaceZ parm) {

    }
}
```

Example 9.1 *Interface Passed to Another Class*

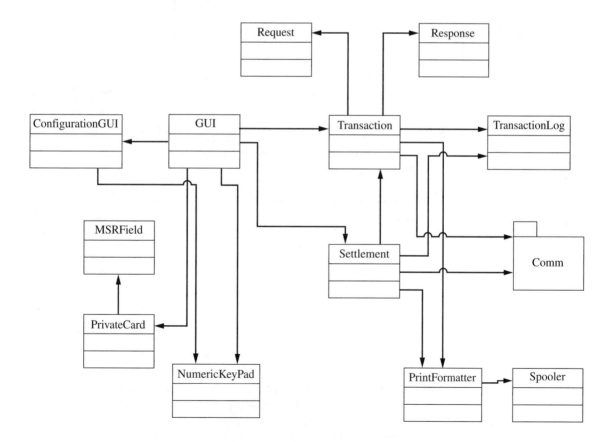

Figure 9.2 *Dependency Graph—First Pass*

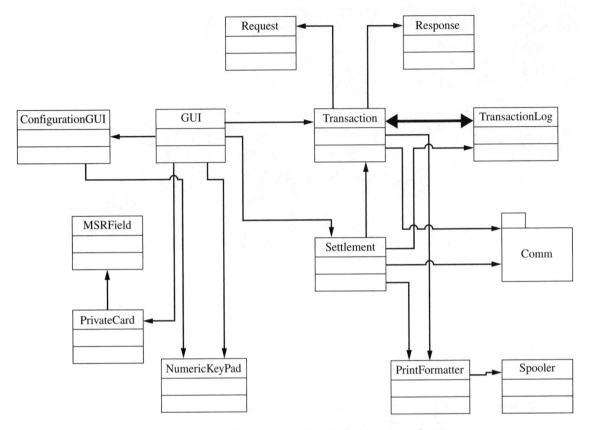

Figure 9.3 *Complete Dependency Graph*

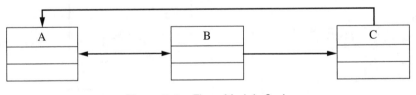

Figure 9.4 *Three Module Cycle*

Once the Dependency Graph has been created, you can begin doing code inspections and testing. The process for doing this is:

1. Inspect and/or test each module that is not dependent on anything other than library modules. Interfaces and Abstract classes can be individually inspected; however, they cannot be separately tested (because they cannot be instantiated). Thus, testing of these modules effectively occurs while testing a concrete class that implements or subclasses this type of module.

2. Inspect and/or test each module whose dependent modules have been inspected or tested.

3. All modules that are in a cycle must be inspected or tested together. This makes inspection and testing much more difficult, which is why these cycles should be avoided if at all possible.

4. Proceed iteratively until all modules have been inspected or tested.

Figure 9.5 illustrates the order in which the modules in our example might be inspected and tested.

Note that if code inspection or testing indicates that you need to change a module that you have already examined, then the examination must pause and you need to go back and inspect/test the changed module before continuing.

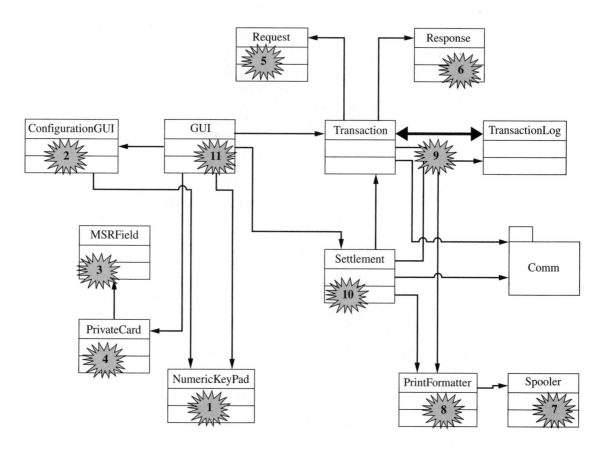

Figure 9.5 *Order of Inspection and Testing*

9.2 Unit Testing

The actual testing performed on each module should test the aspects shown in Table 9.1.

If your system receives messages from another system, you will want to be able to test your system independently from the other system. The best way to do this is to develop a test component that feeds simulated messages into your system.

Especially when you first start testing a program, you will often see Error *Cascading*. This is an effect that one bug leads into error handling code that is itself buggy, leading to more errors. Figure 9.6 illustrates this. The natural temptation is to fix the initial bug and move on. After all, that initial bug was in the code you were testing in the first place. However, that bug in the error handling code is likely in a place that will be rarely encountered in real life. It will also be very difficult to test once the main part of the program is working properly. Thus, a better approach is to start at the end of the error cascade and fix those problems before you fix the problem in the main program. That way, you can more easily find and fix the problems in the error handling code, which are the most difficult parts of a system to test.

In a large complex program, you will run into problems in which you have no idea how things got into the state they did. When this occurs, the best approach is to use a Binary Search to find the problem. Insert a breakpoint or logging event at a point halfway between the point where you know the system was in a good state and where it eventually found itself. Examine the system at that midway point. If the error has already occurred, place a new breakpoint halfway between the known good point and this breakpoint. If the error has not occurred, place a breakpoint halfway between this point and the endpoint. Repeat this procedure until you find the problem.

Table 9.1   *Forms of Unit Testing*

Positive Testing	Testing to verify that the program does what it is expected to do when it receives a valid input
Negative Testing	Testing to verify that the program is robust when it receives unexpected input
Boundary Testing	If a range of values is expected, this tests the low end (and just before it) and high end (and just after it) of the range

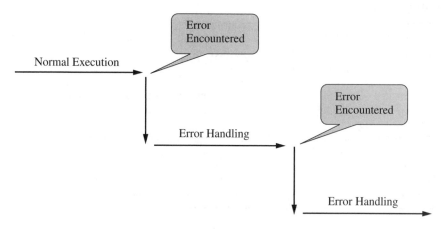

Figure 9.6   *Cascading Errors*

9.3   System Testing

Once the individual components have been unit tested, full-scale System Testing needs to happen. Thorough testing of a software application requires a Test Plan. There are three parts of a Test Plan:

1. What to test
2. How to test it
3. In what order to do testing

System Testing will incorporate the tests performed during unit testing, plus additional testing shown in Table 9.2.

When a software system has separate components being developed by a number of different people, there will always be times when the people have slightly different interpretations of how the components will communicate. Thus, when you first start testing the components together, there will be a mismatch of the messaging protocols. If you have implemented your data validity testing properly, that code will report the errors. Otherwise, the mismatch will cause unforeseen problems somewhere else in your program. At this point, having an event log that records the messages received and transmitted will be vital to resolving the problem.

Table 9.2 *Forms of System Testing*

Functional Testing	Testing to verify that the software properly performs the desired functions. This encompasses the positive, negative, and boundary testing performed during unit testing.
Performance Testing	Verify that the system meets the desired performance goals, especially when it is fully loaded.
Load Testing	Load testing attempts to see if any hitherto unforeseen anomalies occur when the system is fully loaded.
Regression Testing	Testing to verify that an existing feature has not been broken. This is typically performed when the program is changed.

9.4 Exercises

1. An example of a cascading error is an error in the code to analyze a problem and determine corrective action. Explain why this type of error should be fixed early in the development/testing process.

2. Why is the dependency graph useful in deciding what order to do testing?

A

B

C